"I love this creative story that illustrates what a relationship with Jesus based on grace looks like. And the good news is that it's not just a story—it's what the real Jesus longs for with each of us."

—**BRIAN MOSLEY**
President, RightNow Media

"The Path clearly communicates the message of grace to this generation in a profoundly powerful way—including those in my home continent, Africa. The Path is potent, clear, and convicting, and anyone who reads this will be forever impacted. I believe this is essential reading for every young leader who feels the call, the weight, and the responsibility of leadership!"

—**REWARD SIBANDA**
Pastor, Saddleback Church
Senior Director of National Engagement,
Church and Ministry Partnerships, World Vision

"This book is truly a breath of fresh air. It brilliantly weaves in and out of Tal's captivating story of discovering life as it is really meant to be lived. Be prepared to be beckoned even further on the path in your own life as you engage in this beautiful and powerful story."

—**FRANNI RAE CASH CAIN**
Grammy-Nominated Singer & Songwriter, We The Kingdom

"As a filmmaker, I wish thousands of our Gen-Z viewers could read this book. The life principles in The Path have profoundly helped me in my journey."

—**JENS JACOB**
Founding Partner, Sypher Studios, Los Angeles
After Death, The Heart of Man

What Fellow Travelers Are Saying

"As a college president, I know how deeply the questions of identity, purpose, and fulfillment affect this generation of college students. The Path offers the gospel's timeless, powerful answers to these fundamental questions of life, calling us forward into a life of freedom, courage, and peace."

—PAUL J. MAURER, PHD
President & CEO, Montreat College
Author, *The Code of Honor: Embracing Ethics in Cybersecurity*

"This is a must read for anyone who is finding that the world doesn't deliver the fulfillment and happiness it promises. I know, because I tried it all—and found that only Jesus offered me the peace and joy I had always been searching for."

—JEREMY AFFELDT
Three-Time World Series Champion Pitcher, Major League Baseball

"A modern-day Pilgrim's Progress, The Path is a refreshing grace-filled allegory written for such a time as this. We live in a culture where deep shame and broken trust permeate so many relationships. This book invites the reader to take a fresh look at Jesus and to realize we were not made to do this journey alone. Wherever you are in your journey, you will find yourself in one of the characters on these pages. I did. And the questions and reflections are helpful guides on the journey to learn to trust God, yourself, and others."

—JENNIFER JUKANOVICH, PHD
Author, *The Culturally Conscious Board*
Managing Partner, Ambactus Global Solutions: Bringing trust-based solutions to complex problems in governance, education, and international development

"I'm giving this to every young leader I walk with. The Path brilliantly and succinctly sums up what I've been hoping to help them understand for years about who they are, who God is, and why this changes everything."

—DOUG FIELDS
Veteran Youth Pastor, Saddleback & Mariners Church
Author, *Purpose Driven Youth Ministry*
Co-founder & President, DownloadYouthMinistry.com

"Having the privilege to walk alongside thousands of young leaders, I look forward to meeting up with many of them at the rare trailhead of The Path. In a generation desperately searching for identity and purpose, this amazing journey helps all of us answer eight of the most important questions in our lives."

—GRANT SKELDON
Next Gen Director, THINQ
Author, *The Passion Generation*

"As I poured over the pages of The Path, I kept thinking two things to myself. First, 'I wish someone had handed me this book in high school.' My second thought was, 'I cannot wait to read this book with my daughters.' With stunning breadth and precision, The Path beautifully employs metaphor to construct a world compelling the reader to surrender to the immense weight of the love of God. These pictures don't just illuminate one's mind and imagination, but they pinpoint and decipher specific songs of shame lying previously undetected in our hearts. This is a must read for students and adults alike."

—MIKE DONEHEY
Singer & Songwriter, Tenth Avenue North
Author, *Finding God's Life for My Will* and *Grace in the Gray*

Cover & Interior Design by Outskirts Studio
Interior Illustrations by Alex Rodriguez and Pat Malone

TRUEFACE

Produced by **Trueface**
Trueface.org
ISBN: 979-8-9860131-4-5

Printed in the United States.

The PATH

What if the way of Jesus is different
than you thought?

ROBBY : BRITTANY : BENJAMIN : BRUCE
ANGLE : COULSON : CRAWSHAW : McNICOL

Contents

It is a world of magic and mystery, of deep darkness and flickering starlight. It is a world where terrible things happen and wonderful things too. It is a world where goodness is pitted against evil, love against hate, order against chaos, in a great struggle where often it is hard to be sure who belongs to which side because appearances are endlessly deceptive. Yet for all its confusion and wildness, it is a world where the battle goes ultimately to the good, who live happily ever after, and where in the long run everybody, good and evil alike, becomes known by his true name . . . That is the fairy tale of the Gospel with, of course, one crucial difference from all other fairy tales, which is that the claim made for it is that it is true, that it not only happened once upon a time but has kept on happening ever since and is happening still.

—FREDERICK BUECHNER,
Telling the Truth: The Gospel as Tragedy, Comedy, and Fairy Tale

THE CITY

If I find in myself desires which nothing in this world can satisfy, the only logical explanation is that I was made for another world.

—C.S. LEWIS

All good journeys begin with a few good directions, and most exciting journeys include a lot of missing ones. Fellow traveler, as we walk together into the pages ahead we will journey through a world that is like our world but not our world, a land that is everywhere and nowhere. We will meet individuals who are at once impossible, unusual, and yet oddly familiar. We may have known them by another name. We might not know them at all. But in all the familiarity and mystery of this story, we offer the age-old invitation . . .

"Come and see."

∞

It was a crisp fall night. I was eleven.

Like most evenings, I was sketching at the well-worn kitchen table, the fire already lit and my mother kneading dough for dinner. My father walked in, a blast of chilled air coming with him. He greeted my mother, then dropped his leather-wrapped tools on the table next to me. I looked up, startled.

"So, I heard an interesting story today," he began, his eyebrows raised. My mind raced. What had I done? Was this good? Bad? My father was a good man, but when his gaze fixed on me, it usually meant trouble. Otherwise he seemed distant, his mind occupied with work.

"Yeah?" I managed to respond, twirling my pencil uneasily.

"Yeah," he replied, his hand heavy on my thin shoulder. "I heard about the contest at school. For the chicken coop design you drew up. You won!" A wide smile broke across his face as he clapped me on the back. "Well done, Tal! I'm impressed."

I grinned sheepishly, delighted by his words but unsure how to handle the attention. "Thanks," I replied as my mother came over and hugged me, exclaiming her surprise.

"I had no idea those sketches you're always working on would actually come to something," he said, his voice a mixture of pride and surprise as he took his seat at the table. "Hey, they're running a design contest for a new gazebo in the town square. I bet you could win that too."

Yes, I can win that too. I told myself quietly that night as I lay in bed, replaying the pride I heard in his voice.

"I got high marks on my writing test today," I told him two days later, trying to sound casual.

He just grunted, his eyes focused on the chisel he was sharpening. "How's that gazebo design coming?"

"Oh, good." I quietly put my exam paper away. "I was just about to work on it."

I had never designed a gazebo before. I don't think I had ever *seen* one. I stood in the town square each day, trying to picture the new structure, imagining its lines and curves. I considered asking my dad for help, but . . . no. I wanted to show him I could do this.

I sat at the kitchen table and drew each evening.

Sketch after sketch lay crumpled up on the kitchen table, none of them quite right. What was I missing? I thought about going to bed, my eyes heavy and my mind exhausted, but I wanted to get this right. I got up to light another lantern.

It almost became a ritual. Lighting the lantern with shaking fingers to work long into the night. My gazebo design won

me runner-up. Not the winner. Father told me to keep going ... that I had something special. I could see the way his eyes sparkled when he said it. Over time, architecture became my passion. My obsession even.

Then Ricard showed up.

Ricard Beaumont. The premiere architect of Ican. He took me on as an apprentice after seeing some of my sketches. I'd never seen my father so proud. And I'd never been so nervous.

Ricard took me to Ican, our capital city. A place of opulence and importance. Miles away from home and worlds away from what I knew. The gleaming, golden buildings towered majestically, the bustling crowds immersing me in an energy and vibrancy I had never experienced. To my young mind it seemed endless, limitless, full of possibility.

I wanted to belong. To be one of the truly successful here in the heart of everything.

Another year passed and Ricard's rigorous methods of teaching paid off. Like my father, he insisted on perfection. Working for him almost felt like home.

I finally rose to the level of First Key. Your Key level determined everything—your status, your earnings, even where you were allowed to live. Key levels were how you knew where everyone stood. We were a Second Key family, so my lantern stayed on.

Invigorated by getting my First Key earlier than anyone expected, I threw myself into earning my Second Key. It was harder than I thought—more competitive—the wins somehow seeming smaller and less significant the further I rose. When I finally held that gleaming, golden Second Key in my hand, it put me in rooms and on stages I had dreamed about as a kid.

And yet . . . it was only Second Key. The high didn't last long. It was time to forge ahead.

Time passed, sometimes with the adrenaline rush of winning a new architecture contract and sometimes with the cold sweat of a panic attack in the middle of the night. Sometimes the pressure fueled me, and I thrived under it. Other times I felt crushed by its weight. I had the terrible suspicion that I was disappointing people, not living up to my potential. But I knew that if I could just get to Third Key I would be okay.

Autumn leaves turned to snow turned to the new shoots of spring and finally . . . I made Third Key. Ricard threw me a party in the Grand Hall of Ican where only Third Keys were allowed. None of my jealous classmates—who I was certain were hoping to see me fail—could even attend. I was higher than my father had ever been. It had loomed so large for so long; the ledge just above our heads, just out of reach. I knew once my fingers caught it and I pulled myself up I would be able to rest.

But it was on that day—the day when I was supposed to be the happiest and most at peace—that everything I knew to be true started unraveling.

I wandered through the opulent hall, clinking glasses with lavishly dressed strangers. The day before I wouldn't have even been allowed in this room with its towering ceilings and marble pillars. Sunlight streamed through exquisite stained-glass windows depicting the premiere guilds of Ican.

I was with the who's who, the movers and shakers. It was a mix of old families whose roots went back to the founding of Ican and new blood like me who had clawed their way up. All these people had wealth, success, opportunity. They smiled a lot, laughed a lot, and had an easy air I wasn't sure how to replicate. I gripped my crystal glass and told myself to look relaxed.

I tried to take in the moment, to exhale, knowing I had finally *arrived*. I was one of them. This is why my lantern stayed on so many nights—to be in this room. I tried to ignore the voice that still whispered that I didn't really belong. The voice that told me I would be found out as a fake.

I drifted through conversations and congratulations, feeling a bit unsure where to land. Eventually I made my way to the other end of the Hall. It was quieter here, and I could observe the party around me. This party was for *me*. So why did I feel strangely alone—like I was still on the outside looking in? Why didn't I feel happier? *I just need a moment to reset*, I reasoned. *Stop being so anxious*. I headed to an ornate, carved door, hoping it led to a terrace. It was locked. I squinted at the golden letters circling around the keyhole.

Fourth Key Only.

I froze, time slowing around me. Fourth Key? How many keys *were* there? Was there a fifth? A sixth? Endless?

I don't really remember the end of the party. I kept faking a smile and nodding along with strangers, my mind far away. I thought I would finally get to breathe, to rest, but my chest felt tighter than ever. I hadn't truly arrived after all, had I?

I wondered if I ever would. What was the point of all this?

In the months after my Third Key party, I began wandering farther into the outskirts of Ican. I stopped responding to my mother's occasional letters. Ricard told me I was losing my edge, that the others were going to beat me out. But I couldn't seem to care. I was searching for . . . something. That fire that had driven me to Third Key seemed to have burnt itself out, leaving charred, dusty embers in its wake.

I felt uncomfortable in my own skin, like I wanted to escape being *me*. I wasn't sure where I was going or how to get wherever that was. I just wanted to feel okay and not so stressed out. Everyone else seemed to.

One day I wandered all the way to the edge of Ican. I had worked for twelve hours straight the previous day, but my design was mediocre at best. Ricard would rip into me about it if I went to the guild so I just didn't show up.

And here I was, staring down the road into the forest like it could give me answers.

Something caught my eye right at the edge of the pavement. I walked over and pulled vines off an old wooden sign that pointed toward the forest.

Purpose.

My heart beat a little faster. Maybe that's what I was missing.

I heard a rustle above me and looked up. Leaves were dancing on trees high above as the wind picked up.

"Come and see."

Those words rang in my head as I watched the treetops sway. It almost felt like a song. A strange surge flooded my body—a thrill of fear and wonder. An unmistakable draw. An invitation.

Before I realized what was happening, I took a step. Then another.

Then another.

Deeper and deeper into the forest.

A forest clearing opened in front of me, revealing a bustling bazaar. The path I was on split in countless directions with brightly colored canopies and cozy booths all crammed in together. It was colorful and strange and somehow felt much warmer than the manicured streets of Ican. I knew some people left Ican for the forest, but I had never bothered to find out why.

As I started down one of the paths, a young woman waved from a booth with a bright yellow top.

"Welcome!" she beamed.

"Thanks," I replied. I glanced around at the rest of the bazaar. "What is this place?"

"Oh, this is where you choose your purpose. We all have different options, but I'll warn you," she leaned in conspiratorially, "ours is the most fun!"

I laughed. "Okay, so what is it?"

"Adventure," she gestured dramatically at the map behind her. "Travel as much as you can, experience as much as you want—that's what life's all about! We're a pretty free-flowing group. We like to travel light and just soak in the moment, you know? At the end of the day our experiences are really all we have in this life so we try to see as much and do as much as we can." She positively glowed as she talked. I could tell she was a true believer.

"What about family or friends?" I asked, not that I had either really holding me back.

"Well, we're friends with each other. We meet up on trips and plan adventures together. Most of our families understand that this is really what we need to do to be happy, so they're supportive. Of course, some of them tried to give us a different purpose, but," she shrugged, "gotta do what makes you happy, right?"

"Sounds great," I nodded. I liked the idea of adventure and travel, but if I was getting to choose a new purpose, I wanted something a bit more . . . impressive.

I started to move toward the next booth when she called out, "Wait! You can combine it with other ones, you know. If you're doing one of the Build Your Own purposes." She rummaged in a drawer and pulled out a small charm. "Here, most people bring their keyrings from Ican. You can add this if you want. A lot of people like to add Adventure with Humanitarian Work. It's a good mix. But personally, I wouldn't do Humanitarian Work on its own. It's not very fun."

I took the charm from her, squinting at the tiny map etched on it. "Great, thanks. I'll keep that in mind." I pulled out my keyring to add it.

"Third Key, huh?" She nodded at it. "Yeah, not quite what you thought it'd be, was it?"

"Uh, no, I guess not," I replied, taken a little off guard. *She had been a Third Key?* I slid the Adventure charm into my pocket instead of onto the keyring.

The next booth I passed had an all-caps sign that said "FAMILY." Their slogan said, "You only get one family. Love them well!" I just waved when they tried to call me over. I was pretty sure making my family my purpose would just lead to disappointment. In a way it already had.

I stopped and chatted with the attendants at the "Love," "Fitness," and "Fame" booths, and skirted around a whole side street with an ornate banner reading "Religion."

I kept wandering down the well-worn lane, hoping something would stand out to me. I felt sure that this was what I was missing—a bigger purpose. Something outside of myself to live and work for.

I came to a trio of booths that seemed to have a lot of activity. I stopped a man walking by and asked what they were about.

He glanced over to where I was pointing. "Oh, these are the 'Important' booths. See, over on the left you've got 'Be Important.' That's where you need to have influence. People should listen to you and think of you as some kind of expert. You just need a platform. The subject doesn't matter; choose whatever gets you to a place of importance."

"The one on the right is 'Stand Up for Something Important.' That's a huge one; it's got a lot of specialties. You dedicate yourself to standing up for others' rights, for the earth, for yourself, for change in the local councils, you name it. They're all very impactful. I stand up for workers' rights," he told me with a proud smile, pulling out his keyring and showing me the charm. "But I'm working to 'Be Important' too. One day." He shrugged.

"Then in the middle you've got 'Do Something Important.' Again, a really diverse crowd and different ways you can go with it. I mean, they've got scientists working on cures for terrible diseases over there, people running for their local governing seat, crisis and disaster managers, and all sorts of other stuff. A lot of people end up having charms from at least two of the 'Important' booths. They make good pairings."

I nodded, trying to digest the information. This was very different from the guild's culture whose whole goal was just to get ahead of each other. "But . . . " I hesitated, wanting to not sound stupid. "Well, how do you decide what's important?"

He frowned at me. "It's . . . what's important."

"No, no, I know," I replied quickly, feeling the first prickle of embarrassment. "But I mean . . . there are so many important things. How do you decide?" I thought for a moment. "Or what about when two things that both seem important are in conflict with each other?"

He raised his eyebrows at me. "Then I guess you have to decide which is more important to you."

His words sent an unsettled feeling prickling through my body. How could I pick my purpose if I didn't know what was most important? Fighting for peoples' rights was very important, but so was protecting the earth. So was helping the poor. So was protecting small town schools. So were . . . so many things. My anxiety picked back up for the first time since leaving Ican.

I felt a little ashamed that this was difficult for me. How come all these people knew what their purpose was and I didn't? That same feeling of something being wrong with me began to creep in, that velvety, minor key voice drifting through my mind.

I slowly wandered down rows and between booths, collecting charms of places I liked. Where did I really belong?

Eventually I came to a booth set back a bit from the main thoroughfare and close to the river. A man was adjusting a lantern in front of the booth, and a small wooden sign above him read:

THE PATH:
Who Are You Missing?

Guide Notes

What are you searching for?

We're all searching for something. We feel like we're some-how missing "it." We just aren't sure what "it" is. Maybe we need a new job or a new apartment. Maybe if we were just in *that* friend group or with *that* partner then we'd feel good. If we just lost a few more pounds or made a little more money . . .

The list can go on and on.

You have probably seen this search in one of your friends—the one who jumps from relationship to relationship. They get hurt, jump ship, and before they give their heart a chance to heal, they're onto the next person. And while you know that they're looking for peace, love, and fulfillment, you can see that they're miserable.

This is what people do. They go to the next success, the next person, or the next adventure, hoping to find that place where they finally feel okay. Where they belong.

But no matter how strong the emotional connection, even-tually the high fades.

No matter the achievement, the win isn't enough.

No matter the purchase, the joy doesn't last.

No matter the indulgence, we need more and more to get the same feeling.

No matter the adventure, it feels like it's over too soon.

Every milestone we reach, there always seems to be another. What persists is the nagging sense that something's missing.

This quest for fulfillment is as old as humanity. Since the beginning, people have searched deep and wide for peace and happiness. In fact, an ancient king named Solomon wrote an entire journal of all the things he went after in pursuit of fulfillment. He was so wealthy and powerful that he really did have it all. But after all his success, wealth, fame (and wives), he concluded,

> *So I became greater than all who had lived in Jerusalem before me, and my wisdom never failed me. Anything I wanted, I would take. I denied myself no pleasure. I even found great pleasure in hard work, a reward for all my labors. But as I looked at everything I had worked so hard to accomplish, it was all so meaningless—like chasing the wind. There was nothing really worthwhile anywhere.*[1]

Everything the world had to offer, all of its options—Solomon tried them. He could literally have anything he wanted. And guess what? They all came up short. Every single one. Why? Because . . .

» The world can't be enough.
» Other people can't be enough.
» And *we* can't even be enough.

---

1. *Ecclesiastes 2:9-11 (New Living Translation)*

Countless voices will tell you otherwise. They will swear that with just a little more time, dedication, or investment, it will be enough. You can try those voices out. See if they deliver what they promise. But no matter how hard we search, that longing in our soul will always remain unfulfilled.

That is, unless we can understand where it came from.

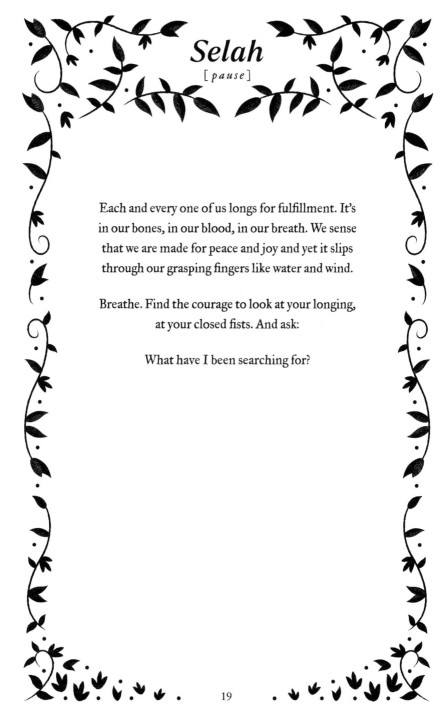

Selah
[*p a u s e*]

Each and every one of us longs for fulfillment. It's in our bones, in our blood, in our breath. We sense that we are made for peace and joy and yet it slips through our grasping fingers like water and wind.

Breathe. Find the courage to look at your longing, at your closed fists. And ask:

What have I been searching for?

THE LEAP

We are born to love, we live to love, and
we will die to love still more.

—ST. JOSEPH CAFASSO

There is a voice that calls to each of us.

Dear traveler, this voice sings to us in a myriad of ways, sometimes in the first light of a new dawn, in the eyes of a friend, or in the tremor of unexpected sorrow. The melody reminds us of the desperate longing that goes past our bodies, past our minds, and into our very souls.

You may have felt this terrible longing and labeled it many things: fear, loneliness, anxiety, heartache. But under all the layers and levels, like a child wrapped in endless blankets, it is the longing for Home.

∞

"The Path," I murmured to myself as I looked at the simple booth set back by the river. I noticed that many of the other passersby waved to the man tending the booth, and he joyfully waved back. He smiled broadly as he saw me.

"Tal, it's so good to see you!"

I was taken aback. "How do you know my name?"

He waved this off good naturedly. "I know a lot of things."

Somehow this put me at ease, even though it wasn't an answer. There was something familiar about him, and yet I felt confident I didn't know him.

I looked around his booth. "Okay, so give me your pitch."

He laughed out loud, and I felt my mouth twitch in a smile. "Straight to the point, aren't you?" he said. "Well, first I'd have to ask, what are you looking for out here?" He motioned toward the bazaar.

I frowned. "I don't . . . I guess I don't know. Isn't this whole place about choosing my purpose?"

He nodded. "And what do you hope you'll get by choosing your purpose?"

"Uh . . . " I frowned again, thinking. "Isn't just finding my purpose enough?"

He shrugged. "Is it?"

"I mean, I want my life to matter," I said, almost to myself. "What I was doing in Ican didn't end up being fulfilling. So, I'm here, wondering if there's another answer."

"So, you're looking for fulfillment?" His brow was knit, his eyes gently curious.

"Do you answer every question with a question?" I responded, slightly exasperated. He just laughed again. I sighed. "Yeah, I guess I'm looking for fulfillment. Or peace. Or rest. Or belonging. I don't know, aren't those what everyone's looking for? Aren't they what's missing? And please don't respond with a question."

He nodded slowly as he looked out over the booths. His gaze was thoughtful. "A lot of these booths will tell you what's missing. And they have wonderful answers. Maybe you're missing service or justice or success or fun. Have you met Mara over at Love? She's great! I really enjoy her. Or have you checked out Morality? You might like that. But Tal, at the end of the day you'll find that all of these wonderful purposes are just different versions of the Keys. It'll come down to *you*."

I watched him study the crowd as I digested what he had —and had not—just said. "So . . . you don't think something's missing?"

A knowing smile spread over his face. "I don't think that's the first question, or perhaps the most important question. I think some*one* is missing."

I squinted at him. "Some*one*? Who?"

He smiled at me, and a warm and bright feeling spread in my chest. "You say you are looking for a purpose, Tal. And purpose really asks the question 'why was I made,' doesn't it?"

I nodded cautiously. "I suppose."

"Now that's an interesting question, isn't it? 'Made.' Because it implies that you don't simply exist as a random collection of molecules. If you were *made* on purpose and for a purpose then you eventually begin asking *who* made you.[1] That's who you're

1. *Genesis 1:27; Psalm 139:13-14*

really looking for, Tal, and who has the answers to your questions. The One who created you *and* your purpose."[2]

I stared at him for a beat of silence. "So . . . what? I'm looking for God?"

"Yeah," he said softly, "God. The One where all the belonging, justice, love, generosity, and joy comes from in the first place.[3] When you try to find those things on your own—even though they're good things—they come up short. You're at the wrong end of the river, Tal. Here in the bazaar you have to work hard to obtain and maintain peace, love, joy, belonging, purpose, you name it. On the Path, God carries you upstream to the source of all those good things—a relationship with him. Instead of it all coming down to you and your efforts, it all comes down to *him*.[4] It's not just another booth or a cause or an interest to add to your keyring. It's a whole other kingdom, Tal.[5] Another way of living from the inside out, not the outside in."

I felt a confusing mess of annoyance, longing, and contempt. Part of me wished that made sense. But most of me knew it didn't.

I laughed humorlessly and muttered, "I guess I should've seen that one coming."

His eyes twinkled like he knew what I was thinking.

"Thanks for your time," I said, "but I'm good. I don't really do the whole religion thing."

He nodded. "Me neither, Tal. Me neither."[6]

I didn't know what to say to that, but I knew I wanted out of this conversation. "Well, see you around." I started to turn

2. *Ephesians 2:10*

3. *I John 4:7; Galatians 5:22; Exodus 34:6*

4. *Romans 5:6-8*

5. *John 18:36*

6. *Matthew 23:1-12*

away and then paused. "Wait, don't you have a charm or something? And what's your name, anyway?"

"No, no charms here, Tal. And my name is Jesus."

I committed to one of the booths: Justice. I eased back on my work with the guild, which irritated Ricard to no end. But I knew I needed more than success in Ican to be happy. I need-ed a purpose, and I found that in fighting for Justice.

I felt exhilarated. Finally I was doing something meaningful! I was committed to something important, and surrounded by such passionate, brave, wise people. It was what I'd been missing, and I finally felt at home. There was a camaraderie in fighting against those who sought to undermine our cause. Sometimes we got a little carried away—I knew that *all* the people on the other side of our chosen issues couldn't be terrible—but the passion reminded me of that old thrill of accomplishment.

There was always some cause to fight for, some wrong that needed righting. I could feel myself getting tired, but I knew I had to keep pushing. The causes were too important. One night as I was walking home from a grueling day at the guild, a friend flagged me down. He told me about a rally he was attending and asked if I wanted to join. I hesitated, wanting to say no, but found myself promising to come. Rest could wait.

Over the next few weeks, I noticed that no matter how hard I tried to attend everything, be involved in every issue, and be outraged at each injustice, I always felt like I was a step behind. Others were doing more, and they were doing it better.

So I pushed harder. But during one meeting, a new member

raised his hand. "But if we defend the leatherworkers," he said, "isn't that harming the ranchers?"

As the meeting slowly unraveled around me, I realized I was feeling exactly like I had in the guild. I wasn't doing enough, or trying hard enough. I was falling behind, and even when I pulled ahead, I was worried someone new would come along and beat me out.

"At the end of the day, you'll find that all of these wonderful purposes are just different versions of the Keys. It'll come down to you." Jesus' words rang in my head. I shook them off. As the minor-keyed voice reminded me, *of course* it was on me. That's called being responsible.

Over the next months as I surrounded myself with these passionate, inspiring people, I continually felt torn. I was trying to convince myself I felt fulfilled and at peace while also trying to figure out what needed to change so I would *actually* feel fulfilled and at peace. I alternated between blaming others for not caring enough about my work and blaming myself for being deficient.

But eventually, I couldn't lie to myself. I was even more ragged and exhausted than I'd been before.

One Saturday morning I headed back down the forest road. Everyone else at Justice seemed to have found their purpose, but I guess it wasn't the right one for me. Maybe I needed something else. As I walked down the forest road, the early light filtering through the swaying branches, I realized I'd been looking for something outside of myself to provide purpose. Maybe that was the problem. I should be looking for something *inside* myself. A colorful corner booth caught my attention as I walked back into the bazaar. In beautiful, mesmerizing letters its sign read "Self-Love."

"Hello, fellow traveler." A beautiful woman greeted me, her smile peaceful and assured. "How is your heart today?"

Without warning, my whole story tumbled out to her. She looked at me with compassion and understanding, her gentle eyes holding mine.

"Finding peace and happiness is connected to your inner spiritual being," she explained. "Purpose follows, but purpose doesn't fix this internal issue. You need to love yourself to find peace."

Yes. That was it. I exhaled deeply, feeling the tension escape my shoulders. She smiled like she understood the relief washing over me.

I committed to Self-Love that day. It felt so good to finally be kind to myself, to find acceptance and belonging right there within my being. I began experiencing more inner congruence and outer awareness. It was incredible.

My work at the guild was important, but not essential. My passion for Justice was good, but not everything. At the end of the day, *I* was all that I truly needed.

Once again, I was exhilarated for a while. I had found the

right path, finally. And the others on this path were peaceful, kind, and grounded. But sometimes . . . things would get confusing.

"So I had to tell her that her friendship was no longer serving me," one of my friends in Self-Love explained one day at coffee. "She had gotten really upset that I canceled lunch last minute, but I needed alone time. How could she not understand? I need to love and take care of myself first. I don't need that kind of negativity in my life."

I told him I understood, trying to hide my confusion and worry. It wasn't the first time that my inner compass had conflicted with someone else's. I just didn't know whose was right.

I came to realize that I still got hurt in Self-Love. And I hurt others as well. The problem was I wasn't sure what to do about any of it. I didn't know how to navigate the pain that life still carried. And while my own inner self was becoming more kind and compassionate, I still felt like something was off. There was a tension between caring for others and caring for myself. Between choosing myself and sacrificing for others. Between wanting myself to be enough, but also needing the love of other people. Something in my inner being felt stuck, no matter how hard I tried to fix it. *I can do this,* I would remind myself. *I am all that I need. Just a little more time and I will be fully at peace.*

But the deeper I dug, the more I became aware that everything rose and fell on me. I had nowhere to rest when the day was hard except with my own self. I had nowhere to go when I was confused and unsure except my own heart, which was often divided. I needed something to stand on that was more than just . . . me.

I got home from a long day at the guild one day and sat down wearily on my bed. I was exhausted from trying to be all that I needed. I leaned back against the wall, closing my eyes.

I was so tired. Why did everything initially feel so good, freeing, and right, and then it would slowly slip through my fingers? At first it would feel like enough, but I always needed more and more to get the same high.

Jesus' words floated back into my mind, unbidden.

On the Path, God carries you upstream to the source of all those good things—a relationship with him. Instead of it all coming down to you and your efforts, it all comes down to him.

My eyes snapped open. I sat frozen in my small room.

It all comes down to him, *not* you.

The words echoed in my head loudly enough that my anxious thoughts were drowned out. Could that really be true?

I stood up, the frozen river in my chest giving way to a gushing torrent. I took a step toward the door. Then another. And another.

Before I knew it, I was running through the streets of Ican with bewildered stares of onlookers in my wake. My feet hit the forest path, and all I could think was that I had to find out. I had to know. I had to try.

And though I was miles away, it seemed like suddenly I was within sight of that little booth by the river.

I could see the smile in Jesus' eyes while I was still a long way off.[7]

I don't know how long Jesus and I walked and talked. Months, certainly. He always felt unhurried, both as we walked

7. *Luke 15:20*

and in our conversations. Some days I would get so frustrated by his answers or his questions or his silence that I would march all the way back to Ican, convinced I was done. But I couldn't stay away. His words would float back to me like a song in the wind, a clear bell drawing me, confronting me, comforting me.

One day while thick clouds drifted overhead, I asked, "Okay, so in your Kingdom, since it's all about love, does that mean nothing bad ever happens?"

Jesus let out a whistle. "No, it sure doesn't. People are there, too, and they still hurt each other. But they have been freed from the curse of sin. They're learning to walk a different way. They're learning that that's not who they really are anymore."

I thought about this for a moment. "So, your Kingdom is not necessarily safe?"

"Hmm," he responded. "Depends what you mean by 'safe.' If by safe you mean easy and that you will never be hurt or afraid, then no. But then that doesn't sound like a great adventure, and it *is* a great adventure." He winked at me. "I am always with you, though, on the Path. Sometimes you can see me, sometimes you can't, but always, always I am with you.[8] You will never travel any of it alone. So, in that sense, it's very safe."

We walked in silence for a while as I mulled this over. "I mean, I like what you're saying and all," I finally said. "But I still don't get why it can't just be one thing I like. You know, like another charm I can add like Justice or Adventure. Honestly, I think you'd have more people if you handed out charms."

He laughed. He did that a lot. "You're not the first person to tell me that, Tal. And some people have made their own charms for the Path to try to add it to their rings. But it's so much more than that. It's a whole different Kingdom. An upside-down,

8. *Matthew 28:20*

strange Kingdom of a wonderful and sometimes bewildering King. It doesn't mix with Ican—it's like oil and water."

"But *why*?"

I asked him this constantly and only sometimes got an answer I understood.

"Because the Path is not 'I Can,' Tal. Rather, it's 'I Can't,' or more importantly, 'He Can.' To enter my Kingdom you have to trust that you can't earn your way into it, no matter how hard you try, no matter how good you think you are.[9] Right now, sin is your master. And no matter how hard you try, you cannot get free on your own. You can't fix your sin—you need me to save you from it and set you free. And it would be my deepest joy if you would let me."

I hated hearing that there was something I couldn't do myself. My whole life had been about proving the opposite. But I also couldn't deny the appeal of the Kingdom Jesus described.

Over the next few weeks, I began to notice that I couldn't get myself to care about the work and amusements of Ican like I used to. My eyes would drift back to the forest, missing Jesus. I couldn't understand it entirely. But I wanted to believe him. I wanted to believe I could trust him.

One day Jesus led me out to a bluff. The sun was bright and warm, and I could hear the light song in the wind that I'd come to associate with his presence. A shimmering river cut through the canyon down below, disappearing under a giant rock formation. I knew beyond it was Jesus' Kingdom. The whole vista was beautiful, but I couldn't really take it in.

My spirit was agitated.

Jesus seemed content to wait, comfortable with my frustration.

9. *Ephesians 2:4-9*

"Honestly, I know this probably sounds bad," I finally blurted out, "but I just don't want to give up my control. I don't! I hate it when you talk about this sin stuff. I don't want you teaching me what's the right way and what's the wrong way. I want to decide that for myself. I want to decide how life works. I want to be able to set the rules. I just—I can't give up control. I can't!" I threw my hands up in front of me, like I was warding Jesus off.

But if I thought this would rattle him, it didn't. His face was full of compassion and understanding. "I hear that, Tal. And I get it. It can feel really scary to trust someone else with *you*. They would have to be utterly trustworthy."

I dropped my hands. This would all be easier if he met my pushbacks with anger, but he didn't.

He thought for a moment as he looked out at the river. Then he turned to study me. "Can I ask you something?"

I sighed. "Sure."

"Why do you want to control your life?"

I picked up a rock and whipped it over the side of the cliff, thinking. "Because then . . . then I don't have to be scared. I don't have to be anxious. If I can control my own life then . . . I can't get hurt."

My words hung in the air as I picked up another rock. *But I tried that,* I thought to myself. *I tried to control my life and I was still anxious and scared and got hurt.*

Maybe you didn't try hard enough, came the velvety hiss.

Maybe I don't want to be my own god anymore, a small, defiant voice responded.

Jesus watched me like he could hear the war in my head. I looked at him and he held my gaze steadily. Something was crumbling inside, making way for something new.

"So to enter your Kingdom, I have to let you take me there. I have to let you rescue me from my sin."[10]

He nodded.

"I can't earn it. Or get myself there."

He shook his head. "I did it all for you, Tal. I already paid the price for your freedom: my very life.[11] And then I came back to life to bring you to the Kingdom myself. To where you belong." He smiled, and added, "And that was no easy thing. I want to do this *for* you because I love you." He closed his eyes, and I saw tears forming in the corners of his eyes. "More than you can possibly fathom.[12] I would do it all again to bring you home."

He opened his eyes and looked at me once more.

My throat tightened as I looked back over the vista. "But I've messed up in so many ways. I've walked away from you . . .

10. *John 14:6*
11. *John 3:16*
12. *John 15:13-16*

many times. I've rejected you. I've even yelled at you. How can I just accept this now?"

He smiled, and held out his hand. "You can trust me, Tal. I've seen it all and then some. There's nothing you could do that would make me walk away. Ever. And there's so much adventure waiting for you beyond."

I knew it was time. In or out.

I could feel something rising up in my chest like the Windsong swirling along the bluff. The sweet and terrible song of acceptance, of surrender.

I had known for awhile. I had just been afraid. But here, standing with Jesus, that fear seemed to dissolve.

Slowly, I stepped up to the edge of the cliff and raised my face, feeling the sun warm my skin. I took hold of Jesus' hand.

His joyful eyes held mine. "Follow me."

And together, we made the Leap.

Guide Notes

What if it wasn't all on you?

The sweetest thing in all my life has been the longing—to reach the Mountain, to find the place where all the beauty came from—my country, the place where I ought to have been born. Do you think it all meant nothing, all the longing? The longing for home? For indeed it now feels not like going, but like going back.

—C.S. LEWIS

Who, or what, do you think God is?

Is God loving, judgmental, all-knowing, worried about our happiness, in charge of hurricanes, hateful, merciful . . . real?

How do you know? Is it based on what feels right to you, what you learned from your parents, heard in school or from friends, saw online, read in scriptures, were told by an influential person, or something else? As we begin to walk down this path with Tal, we are following the God described in a collection of ancient writings called the Bible. These writings help us understand who this wonderful and sometimes bewildering God is that people have followed for millennia. It's important that we determine who God is based on who *he* tells us he is (rather than who *we* want him to be) as we decide whether or not to leap into the unknown and follow him.

So, what do those scriptures tell us?

Two thousand years ago, Jesus of Nazareth lived as a real-life human who claimed that he was also fully God. We're talking Creator-of-the-Universe God. That's a pretty wild claim. As the famous argument goes, he must have either been a lunatic, a liar, or actually who he said he was: God.[13]

There are several records of Jesus' life, both how he lived and the paradigm-shifting ideas and philosophies that he taught. Despite how surprising and counter-cultural most of his teachings were, his life of love and miracles and sacrifice backed them up. He really lived and loved the way he was claiming. Those that lived most closely with him came to the most shocking conclusion of all—that he really, truly, was God-in-the-flesh. It all culminated in him telling them his ultimate purpose: to die and then rise from the dead on behalf of making us right with God. When he did exactly that, his friends and followers gave the rest of their lives (figuratively and literally) to passionately spreading the truths of this Savior to the rest of the world. Even unto death. That's some radical transformation!

Another bizarre dynamic is that these followers were made up of pretty normal and underwhelming people, including some of the outcasts and rejects of society. Certainly not the influential or powerful people you would think he would choose. The records of Jesus' life tell us that one of his best friends while here on earth was a fisherman named

13. C.S. Lewis, *Mere Christianity*, (Harper Collins, 2001), 52.

John—probably a pretty good person to ask what Jesus was *really* like. He got an up-close-and-personal look at Jesus' character day in and day out. Later in his life, when John reflected on his time with God-in-the-flesh, he wrote this:

"Love comes from God . . . God is love."[14]

Notice that this isn't "love is God." But "God is, in his nature, love." John is saying, "Look, I walked with this guy. Camped with him. Prayed, laughed, and cried with him. I got up close and personal. I was there. And if you really want to know what he's like . . . he's love itself."

This is what we're longing for.

We long to experience the peace, fulfillment, and joy that comes from love. We know this not because of a Christian teaching, but because we're living human beings. At the core of our being is the longing for true, full, unmovable love.

And Jesus offers it.

The Love God

But that's jumping to the end of the story. To understand what Jesus offers, we need to go back to the beginning.

Long ago, in a beautiful garden, this Love God created new beings. They were made in his image,[15] meaning they were made to reflect the character of God into the world. They were made to live in relationships, just like God. God knew them, named them, blessed them, delighted in them, loved them, and walked with them each day. The world was good and beautiful.[16]

14. *I John 4:7-8*
15. *Genesis 1:27*
16. *Genesis 1:31*

Take a moment to imagine that. No war, no fear, no poverty. A flourishing earth, bursting with life and joy and peace.

But then.

Then a velvet voice slithered up close to the humans.

Maybe God isn't good.
Maybe he doesn't have what's best for you.
Maybe you could do this without him.[17]

Why was this lie so devastating? Because God didn't create robots. He didn't want robots. He wanted image-bearers who could love, and *love that is forced cannot be love*. We know this intuitively when we worry that someone "loves" us out of obligation rather than freedom and choice. God gave the humans free will to choose to love him back . . . or not.

They chose not.[18]

Every single one of us has chosen the same since, and that has broken the world. It has put us under the curse of sin.

Humans chose to be their own gods, and we are *terrible* gods. This broke our relationships with our Creator, each other, the earth, and even ourselves. Sin (which is anything that is "missing the mark" of love) and shame (the belief that you are a screw-up and undeserving of love) slithered into our world and into our hearts. Ever since, even up until this very second as you read this, we've tried to fix it ourselves. We feel the ache and longing that tells us this is not how this world is supposed to be. We've tried to earn our way back to God, educate our way back to each other, problem-solve our way back to a flourishing creation, and analyze ourselves back to soul health.

17. *Genesis 3:1-5*
18. *Genesis 3:6-7*

Have you noticed something? It's not working. It never has. No matter how much we advance and strive, there are still wars, abuse, greed, poverty, and destruction. Sin is still the master of this world.

God knew we would never be able to make it right ourselves. Despite being the one who was rejected, *he* would have to pay the price to mend what was broken. This was the ultimate expression of his nature of love—he would pay the cost to restore relationship with us.

The price was his life.

The God of the Universe loved you, yes *you*, so much that he stepped down off his glorious throne and entered the broken world. He was born as Jesus. He experienced hunger, laughter, sadness, frustration, delight, deep friendship, terrible rejection, and probably a few stubbed toes and awe-inspiring sunrises. He called to all of us, saying,

> *"Come to me, all you who are weary and burdened, and I will give you rest. Take my yoke upon you and learn from me, for I am gentle and humble in heart, and you will find rest for your souls."* [19]

Many people hated what Jesus was saying. *Especially* the super-religious people. Why? Because it took away their control. He offered something they couldn't earn or accomplish themselves, which threatened their purpose and their religious influence. They killed him, repeating our age-old story of rejecting this God of Love in favor of staying in control. Little did they know, God had planned for this terrible rejection to be our path to freedom. Jesus bore all of *our* sin and shame, taking it

19. *Matthew 11:28-29 (New International Version)*

into his very body that day on the cross.[20] Sin and shame stayed dead. Jesus didn't.

Jesus came back to life. This is the most incredible, shocking, miraculous event that has ever taken place in our world. It changed *everything*. The disciples—the eyewitnesses of this miracle—were so convinced that most of them were later killed because of their belief in Jesus.

Jesus now offers freedom to anyone who will come to him, anyone who will say, "I can't heal myself. I cannot get free from my sin. Only you can, Jesus. You are God and I am not. Help!" He holds his hands out, still giving us the choice to love him or not, to receive his new life for ourselves or not. Jesus tells us that if we will trust him to be our God then sin and shame will be killed in our innermost being. He promises that he will give us a new, true Self, and that he will live with us and within us forevermore.

We will finally be restored to what was intended in that garden and transferred from the kingdom of darkness into the Kingdom of Light.[21]

So what does this really mean for me?

Back to Jesus' good friend John. He records a fascinating interaction early in Jesus' ministry days. Jesus and his ragtag followers were traveling by foot and stopped for a break.

20. I Peter 2:24
21. Colossians 1:13

Strangely, Jesus sends his disciples into town and he sits down alone by a well.

It was midday. Quiet. It was almost like he was waiting for someone.

Soon, a woman appeared on the horizon, coming to get water from the well.

Now, a little context. In this time and culture, Jews (which Jesus was) never interacted with Samaritans (which the woman was). Plus, men didn't talk to women alone unless they wanted a scandal. On top of all of that, this woman was known for having made shall-we-say *questionable* choices in her life. She was getting water alone to avoid more judgment and gossip from the other women in town. She'd had plenty of that.

Needless to say, Jesus was breaking a lot of cultural code here. Scandalously, shockingly so.

The woman was exhausted. She was broken. She'd tried a lot of things to fill her up and nothing seemed to be doing the trick. If we're honest, we've all been there.

Jesus started asking her questions, just like with Tal. That seemed to be his favorite approach to almost anyone. Eventually while sitting at this well he told her:

> "Everyone who drinks this water will be thirsty again, but whoever drinks the water I give them will never thirst. Indeed, the water I give them will become in them a spring of water welling up to eternal life." [22]

22. *John 4:13-14 (NIV)*

Jesus is talking about how the things we chase always seem to come up short, the experience Solomon called "chasing the wind"—that quest for fulfillment that always seems just out of reach. We keep thinking the next thing, the next friendship, partner, job, city, whatever, is going to fulfill us. But it falls flat, leaving us feeling just as terrible as before. Or we get the initial high from something new, but it just doesn't seem to last unless we do more and more. This woman understood that to her weary bones. Jesus is saying,

"You want fulfillment? It's me."

Jesus is the peace, fulfillment, and rest that we are longing for. *He* is the well that never runs dry. When we surrender to him, he fully fuses with us, offering his love, joy, peace, patience, kindness, goodness, gentleness, and self-control as a bubbling-up-spring every moment of every day.[23] It's not a trickle that depends on our behaviors. It's not a water pump where we get more out if we put more effort in. It's a gushing, drenching fountain of love![24]

This isn't found in our learning, earning, or striving. It's only found in our *receiving* what Jesus did for us. Full stop. We come to the end of ourselves, and instead receive the extravagant fullness of God.

The woman at the well experienced this extravagant love on that day, long ago on a dusty road in Samaria. Her world was both shattered and restored in that moment. In one encounter,

23. *Galatians 5:22-23*
24. *1 John 3:1*

she was fully dignified—fully worthy of love and respect. She finally found what she had been looking for.

The way of Jesus is not a philosophy, a moral guidebook, or a nice add-on to our lives. It's an entirely different Kingdom, where he reigns with love. It's an entirely different reality.

To each of us, Jesus holds out his hand on that ledge, asking us to trust him.

Will we leap?

Selah

One day, you will be weary.

You will have run to the end of what your human body can carry. You will have tried to untie the knots of your soul until your fingers are bloody and brittle. You will have scaled and fought and wept and raged and found that it still did not satisfy the longing in your soul.

Today may be such a day.

If you are weary enough to sit down on this dusty road, notice the One who settles beside you. Who offers you a cool drink for your raw throat, bread for your gnawing stomach.

What does he want you to know?

THE TABLE

What if you truly are who God says you are? After all, when our view of ourselves disagrees with God's view of us, who's right?

—ANDREW FARLEY

We each have a melody that plays quietly in our minds, telling us who we are.

There are many key changes throughout our lives, even throughout our days. Sometimes the song tells us we are successful, powerful, and good. Sometimes it tells us that we are worthless, unlovable, and alone. And no matter how many times we try to fix this melody, rewind it, rewrite it, it continues to shift like the ocean in a storm. But the One who knew us before we knew ourselves is like the horizon, steady in the waves, telling us who we truly are over and over:

"You are mine.

You are mine.

You are mine."

∞

The first thing I noticed was the lapping of water against my skin. The second was the grit on my face like wet sandpaper. The third was a voice I didn't know.

"Tal!"

Groaning, I rolled onto my back. I cracked open my eyes and the blurry outline of a man came into view, running toward me. I shut my eyes tight again against the blinding sun, but the next thing I knew he was scooping me up out of the water and setting me on my feet. He brushed the sand off my skin, quickly wrapping me in a towel as I tried to get my bearings.

Where am I? I tried to remember what had happened. The last thing I remembered . . .

I jumped.

We jumped.

The man placed his hands on my shoulders, bringing my gaze to his.

"I have been waiting for you," he told me, his eyes brimming with joy. His voice was warm and strong, reminding me of evening fires and towering oak trees. "I knew my Son would bring you."[1]

Son.

Jesus suddenly walked up beside us—also soaking, also beaming at me. "Welcome to my Father's Kingdom, Tal!"

This new person was unmistakably royal. He wore deep purple robes with gold embroidered along the hem, and yet he seemed utterly unconcerned with the water slowly seeping

1. *I Peter 3:18; John 10:27-29*

into the fabric. The crown on his head somehow looked comfortable, like it was as natural on him as a stag's horns.

The King smiled deeply. "I'm so glad to welcome you home, my child. I am Abba. Father."[2]

That same strange sensation—that Windsong that was either within me or around me or both—rose up in my chest so strong and beautiful it nearly ached.

Father. It sounded right.

"Nice to meet you," I managed to choke out. I looked back at the giant rock I had passed under. I felt different. I felt . . . new.

Jesus followed my gaze to the rock. "'When we went under the water, we left the old country of sin behind. When we came up out of the water, we entered the new country of grace—a new life in a new land!'"[3]

"I've been preparing for you for a long time," Abba said quietly. I felt my brow furrow. I could hardly believe he knew my name, let alone that he had been . . . preparing for me. Planning for me.

Before I could ask anything more, his smile brightened. "Come!" He clapped his hands. "I'm sure you are starving." Abba led me toward the thick trees that lined the river's beach, Jesus walking beside me. It was comforting to have him close by in this new place.

"Where am I?"

Abba responded as he walked. "You passed under the Rock, Tal.[4] You're in a whole new Kingdom. My Kingdom to be exact," he said, laughing. "And now yours, too. Or, as a friend of mine

2. Galatians 4:6-7
3. Romans 6:3 (The Message)
4. Matthew 21:42

once said, 'You are over the Edge of the Wild now, and in for all sorts of fun wherever you go.'"[5]

I didn't know what that meant, but I knew I was far, *far* from Ican. Strangely, that thought didn't scare me. *Over the Edge of the Wild* . . . yes. That captured the feeling perfectly.

We were now winding through the trees. The boughs above seemed to light up from the glint off Abba's crown. The smell of food hit me, smokey and rich, and my mouth immediately began to water. I heard laughter drifting over us, calling us onward.

We entered a clearing set with a giant, colorful tent canopy laced with vivid flowers and flanked by intricate lanterns. A long wooden table stretched across the ground that was so laden with food I thought it might collapse. I gaped at the sight, stopping in my tracks.

People were everywhere, dancing and laughing. There had been parties in Ican, but they never came close to this. This felt somehow consequential, yet at the same time relaxed. There

5. J.R.R. Tolkien, *The Hobbit* (Harper Collins, 2007), 129.

was an ease, a naturalness, to everything these people were doing. Like they were truly just enjoying themselves. I'd never seen anything like it.

I felt Jesus nudge me forward, and my feet started moving again. As we stepped into the clearing, faces turned toward us with smiles lighting up each one. The whole clearing suddenly broke into thunderous applause.[6]

I turned to look at Jesus and Abba—surely this was for them. But they were beaming at me too, clapping with the rest as tears ran down their cheeks.

They were cheering for . . . me.

I was embarrassed to feel my eyes stinging as I blinked back tears.

"What is this?" I whispered. Clearly I was missing something.

"They're so glad you're here," Jesus said quietly, squeezing my shoulder.

"But I haven't done anything," I whispered back, a little pan-icked. There had been galas in Ican, but they were reserved for the highest achievers and royalty. I was neither.

"Just being you is enough," he replied. "You are loved and delighted-in, simply because you are *you*."

Something seemed to crack in my chest, breaking open wonderfully, painfully. Part of me reeled back, pushing against the joy that was pouring in from all directions. I didn't deserve it. That velvety voice murmured that these people didn't really know me yet, and once they did this would all go away. Maybe Abba thought I was someone different than I was.

But the voice was drowned out by the clear melody of the Windsong swelling in the clearing. The love was too loud. I

6. *Luke 15:7*

looked back at Jesus. He nodded like he knew exactly how I was feeling.

I turned back to the crowd with so many kind and bright faces whistling and cheering, and I was struck by the difference from the Grand Hall. *They're cheering for* me. *Not for something I've accomplished. Not for some way I've impressed them. Just for . . . me.* I struggled to take it in.

Abba held his hands out, calling for quiet.

"My dear ones, today we welcome my child Tal to our family and to our Kingdom. You have each passed under the Rock and through the water with my Son, and you know how this changes the very essence of who you are. You are alive-for-the-first-time people; new, beloved, and forever my children and heirs to my Kingdom."[7] Suspense seemed to rise in the clearing as he paused. "It is time for Tal to receive the Crest."

Jesus produced a small gold Crest from his pocket as he stepped up to me. It felt as though everyone in the clearing was holding their breath. My skin tingled as every eye trained on the glinting object. "Tal, you are a beloved child of the King. This sacred, holy Crest is gifted to you, not earned. It is a symbol to remind you of what happened to you when you went under the water, and who you now are.

I looked into his eyes, finding love there. "*What* happened to me?" I asked, even as I recognized that somehow . . . I was different. It wasn't just a feeling; it was much deeper than that.

"I gave you a new heart. I took out your old heart—disconnected from me, striving to make life work for itself, constantly seeking its own way[8]—and I gave you a new heart, a heart like

---

7. Romans 8:15-17; 1 John 3:1
8. Jeremiah 17:9; Isaiah 53:6

mine.[9] Your innermost being has changed, Tal. That's what the heart on your Crest means." He looked down and pointed to the gold object. "You have a heart of love now, of trust, a heart that is fully connected to me. I've come to live *in* you. That's what this symbol in the middle of your new heart means."

"But what do you mean, come to live *in* me?" I replied. "You're . . . well, standing right there."

Jesus smiled. "True, but my Spirit is living in your new heart. Your spirit and my Spirit are now joined together as one.

You may not see me at times, but this Crest will remind you that your heart is fused with mine no matter where you are.[10] This isn't something you can achieve, win, mess up, or lose. It is yours forever. I went down to death and came back up to life so that I could give you this gift."

"Just like passing through the water," I said quietly. Death to life.

He smiled, nodding. "When you died to yourself and be-

9. *Ezekiel 36:26; Romans 6:17-18*
10. *Matthew 28:20*

came alive in me, who you are was changed. Your choice to trust changed your very essence."

Jesus gently touched the Crest to my chest. Painlessly, it branded into me. I touched it gingerly, tracing its lines. "Forever?" I looked up at him.

Joy shone out from him. "Forever."

The crowd broke into cheers again, some taking up instruments and others flooding toward the table. Abba now put his hands on my shoulders, speaking for only me to hear. "You're my child, Tal. And just like Jesus will never stop being with you, I will never stop being your Father. There is nowhere you can go where I won't be there to help you, guide you, support you, empower you.[11] There is no emotion too big for me or problem too small for my care. And nothing—*nothing*—can change that.[12] You will have seasons when you don't feel this is true, or when you struggle to believe it. Even then, this Crest is here to remind you of who you really are and what is true. You are beloved, and you belong. You are now one with us."

He held my gaze for a moment, and I was struck again by the gentle authority in his voice. I simply nodded. I didn't yet fully understand all that he was telling me, but I felt its significance in my bones.

"Now it's time for a feast!" Abba ushered me further into the clearing and toward the table. As we walked, people high-fived and hugged me as though I was an old friend returning from a long journey. At first I felt awkward. I didn't know these people at all. But soon I started to laugh with them, letting the crowd's joy sweep me along as more hugs poured in.

Eventually I made it to the table, piled more abundantly

11. *Psalm 139:7-12*
12. *Romans 8:31-39*

with food and drink than I'd thought when I first arrived. Abba led me onward until we were at the head of the table. Jesus took his seat at Abba's right hand, motioning me to his left.

"Are you sure I can sit here?" I asked uncomfortably.

"Absolutely," Abba responded decisively. "You are an heir and a delighted-in child. Where else would you sit?"

Over the next hour I listened to the conversations around me. Some people were cracking each other up. Others listened intently. Some just leaned back in their chairs, relaxed, like the older woman across from me.

"It's a big family," Jesus winked.

"Apparently." I laughed a little, looking down the table. Everyone looked different, but the light in their eyes seemed the same. *Joy*, I thought. Pure and unhindered.

"And 'family' is the right word." The woman across from me leaned forward as she spoke, her eyes twinkling. "We sometimes fight, or misunderstand each other, or get grumpy. But at the end of the day, we love each other because that's just who

we are now. We're all kids of the same King who went to the ends of the earth to rescue us and bring us home. And now we have a heart like his, one that naturally moves toward love."

I thought of the quiet dinners in my home. I thought of my father, usually distracted and distant. My mother, doing her best but unwilling to challenge him. That prickly feeling that I needed to do something impressive to be worthy of his love and attention.

I looked back at Abba, who was resting his chin on his hand, just smiling at me. Enjoying watching me take it all in. And for the moment, I didn't feel like pushing back. He saw *me*. He loved me, inexplicably, just because I was me. I shook my head slightly. A wonderful and sometimes bewildering King indeed. A true Father.

"Okay, so . . . what is this place?" I asked him, my curiosity starting to rise as my food settled.

Abba spread his hands wide as he leaned back in his chair, "This is my Kingdom Table. This is where you first discover and enjoy who you are now. You aren't who you were, Tal, even on your worst day. You left that identity behind. *This* is who you are now. Fused with my Son, Jesus, with all of his wisdom, power, and love bubbling up in you like a fresh spring." He looked around, and then stood. "Let's walk a bit, shall we?"

We wandered through the clearing, Abba introducing me to people as we passed. Soon we were walking through the trees on the edge of the clearing. A woman passed us by, traveling away from the warmth of the table.

"Mara," Abba called kindly. "Won't you come sit with us?"

"Oh, no, thank you," she replied quickly, avoiding eye contact. "You see I'm very behind in reading the holy scriptures. And twice this week I ate too much. I know I need to get back to abiding in Jesus. I'll come join just as soon as I get those things taken care of."

"Mara, you are always abiding in Jesus. You and he are one. You are in him. He is in you. Don't you remember when we gave you your Crest?" He reached out to gently tap it. "You don't need to take care of anything before you come and enjoy my Table. Your seat is waiting for you on your best days and your worst days."

"Yes, yes, I know," she replied distractedly, "I'm sure I'll come soon."

I frowned as she hurried off.

Abba watched her go, sorrow lining his face. "Tal, remember this moment in the days to come. My children so easily go back to living like they're in Ican. They are afraid they need to measure up, keep up, and work hard enough to *earn* their seat at my Table. They stay on the fringes of the joy and delight I offer them, longing for the warmth but not believing that they deserve it until they've done enough. Shame tells them that it can't possibly be this simple—that I've done it all for them. It breaks my heart, Tal."

Mara was not the only one we encountered in the forest. There were many who belonged at the Kingdom Table who did not join us. Some proclaimed that they preferred to eat alone. Others grew wide-eyed at Abba's gentle approach, convinced that they had failed too often and too recently to rejoin the Table. Still others were suspicious of their own Crest, proclaiming that, "It can't be that easy." And with each one, Abba would gently invite them to come and enjoy his food, drink, and presence again.

Abba smiled down at me, sensing my concern. "Don't worry, Tal. They will come back to my Table in the end. But for now, come. I have so much more to share with you."

What if you already are who you wish you were?

"Who am I?"
"What do I think of myself?"
"Why does my life matter?"

These are the questions that drive most of our lives. At their deepest level, the booths Tal encountered at the bazaar are proposed solutions to these questions. They promise fulfillment and an identity. We come to define ourselves by our careers, talents, influence, family, friends, passions, and more. We may shape our identity as an artist, social justice advocate, spouse, business leader, or something else.

For a while, these identities seem to deliver because they are usually good things. But they require a lot of work to maintain and bring a lot of pressure. And though they may give us a temporary high of fulfillment, it doesn't stick. It feels like we get all glitter and no gold. All sizzle and no steak.

That's because these things are supposed to be the arenas in which we live, not the core of who we are. They were never meant to be our true identity. They cannot bear that weight.

Who You Are Now

What Tal just received—what we all receive when we take the leap with Jesus—is not like these hamster-wheel, self-effort identities. Rather, we receive a new **core** identity.

This new identity:

» Changes the core of who we are forever.
» Is received, not earned.
» Transforms us from the inside out, not the outside in.
» Never expires, wears thin, or is in danger of being lost.
» Affects every area of our lives.

While all the other identities take time and effort for you to secure, *this identity becomes yours instantaneously.*

While all the other identities are ultimately at risk, *this core identity is permanent—never at risk.*

While all the other identities are secondary, *this core identity can help all your unique identities flourish.*

If our new identity comes from God and isn't something we ourselves produce, we'd better let God tell us what it is. It can be tempting to return to our "I Can" ways and choose to define ourselves. But the miraculous, challenging, freeing truth of God's Kingdom is that *he* now defines us.

The Bible says that when we place our trust in Jesus, we

become new creations. But what does that really mean? What's actually new about us?

Our new core identity has two parts, corresponding to the two parts of the Crest that Jesus gave Tal.

Part 1: Born of God

First, when we place our trust in Jesus, God places within us a completely new heart. Jesus told a man named Nicodemus that this was essential to entering into God's kingdom.[13] God removes our old, sinful heart—forever at odds with him[14]—and births within us a new spirit, a new heart.[15]

This new heart is our core identity. We're not talking about who we will be one day in heaven or who we can supposedly make ourselves into if we do enough religious stuff. Rather, if we were able to peer inside to our true self, our inmost being, what would we find?

We would find a person who is holy, righteous, and spotless. The Bible says that we are now "sharers in the nature of God!"[16] We know that this is true because the Holy Spirit birthed our new heart within us, and he cannot give birth to anything that doesn't share his nature.

This is what God sees when he looks at you. He doesn't see this because he's fooling himself into thinking we're this way. Or because he counts us to be this way, even though he knows we really aren't. No, God sees us this way because that's how we truly are now.

13. *John 3:3-6*
14. *Jeremiah 17:9*
15. *II Corinthians 5:17*
16. *II Peter 1:4*

We are God's children, not just because he has adopted us (though he has done that), but because he gave birth to us. Over and over again the Bible says that we have been "born of God."[17] No wonder we are the righteousness of God in Christ![18] We were (re)born that way. In the depths of our being, we are no longer sinners. We are righteous saints.

Our behavior, however good or bad it might be, doesn't change what is now true about us. Our identity is based on our birth. God of course wants our identity to affect our behavior, but our behavior does not affect our identity.

So the first part of our new core identity is this:

We are a child of God, born of him, and a righteous, holy, new-creation saint.

Part 2: God's Dwelling Place

The second part of our core identity is that we are now the place where God lives. This is what God promised his people long ago, what Jesus promised and prayed for, and what the Apostle Paul said was the main message God gave him to preach: that Jesus himself now lives in us.[19] We are the permanent dwelling place of God himself, so that through us, God might express his own life and love to all the universe. Paul captured this reality perfectly when he wrote:

17. John 1:13; 1 Peter 1:23; 1 John 4:7
18. II Corinthians 5:21
19. John 14:16-20, John 17:20-26, Colossians 1:25-27

I have been crucified with Christ, and it is no longer I who live, but Christ lives in me. And the life which I now live in the flesh I live by faith in the Son of God, who loved me, and delivered himself up for me.

—GALATIANS 2:20 (ESV)

In this one verse, Paul captures the whole thing:

1. We are God's beloved. We are so loved by God that Jesus himself died for us.
2. We are a completely new creation. The old us died with Christ. We are a new self.
3. Jesus himself is the one living his life in us, expressing his life through us.
4. We live by trusting. We do not trust in ourselves and our ability to make the Christian life work, but we trust in Christ—God himself who now lives in us.

If we add the two parts of our identity together, we get this:

I am a child of God, born of him, and a righteous, holy, new-creation saint in whom God himself lives, expressing his very life through me.

But what about when I still sin?

Let's ask the obvious question: if we are now holy and righteous, why do we still sin? God gives a very specific answer to that question. When we became alive in Jesus and took the leap with him, we died to sin.[20] The power of sin was removed from our inner being. We aren't joined to it anymore. In the depths of our being, we no longer really want to sin.

But, sin didn't leave us altogether. It's still a power that exists in these mortal bodies we have, and it can still influence us. It's not who we are, and it's no longer what we really want, but it can deceive us into thinking we do.[21]

Our free will didn't go away when we accepted Jesus and he made us new. We can still try to live as if we are our old, dead self. Those patterns of living and responding, thinking and feeling have been with us a long time, and they feel natural. They are *not* natural to the new you, but they feel that way. But the beautiful truth is that these behaviors do not change who you are.

You are not defined by your behaviors. You are defined by God.

If you continue to live as if you are your old self, you'll be miserable. Sure, it will be fun for the moment—sin delivers its promised pleasure. But it's now the opposite of what your inner being really wants, so it will grate on you in a way that feels like sand between your toes. It will make you feel anxious, uneasy, insecure, and defensive, and you'll get less and less pleasure out of it.

20. *Romans 6:1-14*
21. *Romans 7:17-23*

So when you find yourself living in the old way, you can truthfully tell yourself,

I'm not acting like myself. This isn't who I really am. I forgot for a time, or it felt scary or difficult to believe who God says I am. But I am going to agree with God that he defines who I am. I am not defined by my behavior, thoughts, or feelings. Help me remember who I really am, Jesus.

He already covered all your sins, past, present, and future.[22] He knew that this moment would come.[23] And he still said, "You're worth my very life, dear one."

As someone who has been made new, you can think of yourself as a gangly 14-year-old who just grew a foot over summer break. Your old clothes don't fit. Your new clothes are a completely different shape and size than you're used to. You are not yet very coordinated, knocking things over with your newly-long arms and hitting your shin on coffee tables.

You don't know how to use this new, tall body. It's yours, it's done, it's true down to your DNA. But it will take time and intentionality to experience what it's capable of.

That is what your new identity in Christ is like. It's new. It's complete. Jesus is fused into your very DNA. But this doesn't mean we aren't clumsy with it or have moments where we live as though we're still a foot shorter. It will take time to learn how to live in this new reality. But thanks be to God! The reality doesn't become more or less true depending on our coordination.

22. Romans 8:1
23. Psalm 139:16

Enemy Tactics

Mysteriously, not all keep feasting at the Table once they've been there.

Many who already possess this new identity stumble through life like they never got a Crest. They're always looking over their shoulder, darting glances and ignoring what God says is true about them. They forget their new core identity and therefore hide in fear that if they were truly known by others they would be exposed as unlovable and unworthy. And so they must hide, strategize, and cover up for what they're afraid is true.

What a tragedy.

They are already loved, but the velvet voice of the enemy tells them they are only worthy of love if they work hard. They are already accepted, but he whispers to perform for admiration. They are already chosen, but he plants the fear that they are alone. As Jesus says of the enemy, "When he lies, he speaks his native language, for he is a liar and the father of lies."[24]

Sometimes these lying voices are more subtle, like those with religious overtones. They say things like:

» This is who you will maybe be one day, with enough work.
» You've changed in theory, but not in reality.
» You need to work hard to stay close to God.
» Your true heart is (still) deceitful above all and desperately sick.

24. *John 8:44b (NIV)*

These sound noble, almost humble. But they are just pride wrapped in a prettier package. They disregard God's finished work of your new, Spirit-birthed, in-dwelt heart. They put you back in control. There is a quiet, "Now, don't relax!" laced into their words. The lie from these voices comes in two parts: they do not see God as he is, nor do they see you as you are.[25]

Jesus ended religion. Religion says, "You have to work hard to become a new person." Jesus says, "I will make you new, all by myself. Since you cannot possibly work hard enough to become new on your own, I'll do that work for you. You can stop trying to be good enough. The pressure's off."

If you find yourself wandering in the woods rather than enjoying the Kingdom Table, don't worry. We've all chosen the fringes over our rightful seat many times. Relax. Breathe. Grace specializes in imperfection. And the Father is always inviting you to come enjoy. He's saved your seat right next to him.

25. John Lynch, Bruce McNicol, and Bill Thrall, *The Cure, Third Edition* (Trueface, 2016), 2.

I sat beside a large fire and held my hands out toward the flames, listening to the crack of the wood and the soft murmur of conversation around me. Peace. Was that what this was?

I didn't know how long I had been camped at the Kingdom Table. Time seemed to pass differently here.

Movement next to me announced the arrival of Jesus, sitting down on my log. He had been right; sometimes I wouldn't see him physically for a day or two. But in those times I would do what he had taught me—touch the Crest and remind myself that he was as close as the brand on my skin. Closer, in fact. He lived within me, even as he moved and worked around me.

"Your journey continues tomorrow, Tal," he told me, grabbing one of the sharpened sticks to roast an apple over the flames. "I've already packed you a bag."

"I don't just stay here?" I replied, surprised.

He shook his head. "You can always, always return here. You always belong here. And someday you'll probably be back here celebrating someone else making the Leap! But Tal, I have *so much* for you. So much for you to experience and discover— about me, about yourself, about others. There are some grand adventures ahead. They will sometimes get dark or difficult, but I will always be with you." He tapped my Crest. "I have set my song in your heart, and it will lead you."

I looked around the circle at my new family, and part of me didn't want to leave. It was comfortable and comforting here. I was experiencing peace for maybe the first time. But Jesus' words also stirred something in me: a longing and wonder for what he had for my life.

So I nodded. "When should I be ready?"

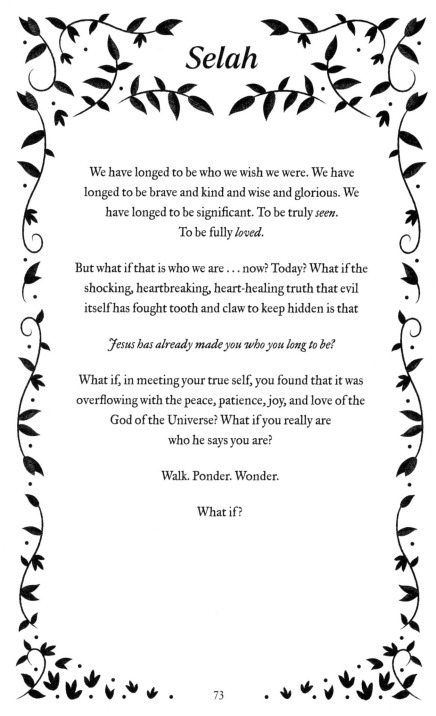

Selah

We have longed to be who we wish we were. We have longed to be brave and kind and wise and glorious. We have longed to be significant. To be truly *seen*. To be fully *loved*.

But what if that is who we are . . . now? Today? What if the shocking, heartbreaking, heart-healing truth that evil itself has fought tooth and claw to keep hidden is that

Jesus has already made you who you long to be?

What if, in meeting your true self, you found that it was overflowing with the peace, patience, joy, and love of the God of the Universe? What if you really are who he says you are?

Walk. Ponder. Wonder.

What if?

THE CAVE

Faith is not believing in my own unshakable belief.
Faith is believing an unshakable God when everything
in me trembles and quakes.

—BETH MOORE

W e have long been under a curse.
This curse has fractured our hearts and warped our bodies, twisting our minds into thorn bushes that make us wince and bleed. We struggle and strive and cry out for someone to save us from this plague we have lived under all our days.

Dear traveler, Jesus has broken your curse. A new, holy heart now beats in your chest: steady and glorious and strong. But long have we limped. Long have we listened to our tangled minds. Be gentle with yourself as you learn to walk as a Loved One.

And when you find yourself walking again in your curse-ways, remember how you came to this new land.

"Trust Me."[1]

1. John 14:1

∽

The morning was cool and crisp with dawn just starting to filter through the forest canopy. Abba and Jesus walked with me along the Path, our steps softly rustling the leaves along the trail.

I looked up at Abba.

"Will I see you further on?"

He smiled a little mysteriously. "I am everywhere, Tal.[2] And I take many forms."

I frowned, unsure what that meant.

The trees thinned and gave way to a grassy plain with towering mountains in the distance. We paused.

"Remember who you are now, Tal," Abba told me, pulling me in for a big hug. "You are mine, and you can trust me."

I looked up at him and nodded. Excitement and nerves fluttered in my chest.

Jesus and I walked forward on the narrow path that lead through an open field. The tall grass rolled and shifted with the wind like a green ocean. Birds dove in and out of the long stalks, picking up their meals for the day and calling out to one another.

At one point, I turned to comment on them to Jesus. But he was gone. *No, not gone,* I reminded myself even as panic flashed. *He's right here. He's with me. He's in me.*[3] I rested my hand on the Crest. My heart settled.

I continued walking toward the base of the distant mountain range, enjoying the feel of the open air. The Windsong was

2. *Psalm 139:7-10*
3. *Galatians 2:20*

loud in my heart. Or my ears? I still couldn't quite figure it out. Occasionally I would touch my Crest and remind myself, "I'm a child of the King, and he's a good Father."

I believed and didn't believe. I knew and didn't know. Others at the Kingdom Table had told me this was how it usually went, moving from my head to my heart. From thinking to experiencing. From knowing to *knowing*.

Something had happened to me, and now everything was different. Of that I was sure. There was still so much I didn't understand, so much I struggled to grasp, but it was thrilling at the same time. This hike to who-knows-where, for example. Before, I would have been worried about where it was leading or trying to speed up getting there. Maybe wondering if I was ahead of the pack or behind it.

But instead I was whistling and laughing at the birds as they chased each other around, confident that something good was afoot.[4] After all, I was a kid of the King out for an adventure.

I was surprised at the little piece of sadness that then floated through my chest. *I wish I had felt this way with my dad.* My thoughts slowed as I let my hand trail through the tall grass, still dewy from the dawn. *I wish my parents had experienced this for themselves.*

I wondered what would have been different. For them. For me.

Loud singing startled me out of these thoughts, drifting over the field. In the distance, I saw a man walking straight toward me with several sheep following behind him. The closer he got, the larger he appeared. His broad shoulders and long, wild hair and beard reminded me of a bear-turned-human. He waved me toward him. "Come on, Tal! Come meet the children."

4. *Romans 8:28*

He knew my name? *Of course he does,* I smiled to myself. As I got closer, the Windsong seemed to reverberate off his tall, burly frame.

He looked at my Crest. "Welcome to the family, child! My name is Rohi."

His vivid green eyes were captivating, full of peace and joy like a merry, mossy river. "Nice to meet you, Rohi. That's an unusual name. What does it mean?"

He opened his hands and looked around him as though he expected my answer.

I paused. "Uhhh, lover of sheep?"

Rohi's thunderous laughter burst over the field as he let his head fall back. It was infectious. Soon I was belly laughing at his unabashed, ridiculous laughter. I couldn't remember the last time I'd laughed like that.

A few minutes later he wiped his eyes, sighing. "Ah, that's a good one. I've never heard that before." He looked toward me. "And it's good to hear you laugh out loud, Tal. It's been awhile."

He chuckled again as he looked at his sheep. "Come on, children." He put his massive arm around me. "Walk with me, Tal."

He began leading us toward the mountains. The herd quietly picked their way behind us. He smelled like leather and new grass, and felt like ease and energy all at the same time. Skillfully he navigated us around large boulders and past muddy patches, calling out to the sheep behind us as we went.

"Have you heard any of the songs written about me, Tal?" He asked as he looked out over the plains. The bright green of the grass reflected in his eyes. I shook my head.

"A dear friend of mine used to be a shepherd, too. And out in plains like this he would write about me. One I really love starts like this:

"The Lord is my shepherd,
I have all that I need."

I smiled, hopping over a ditch that Rohi pointed out. I had thought he felt like Abba, and my suspicion was beginning to grow. The words were comforting as the Shepherd led me forward.

"He lets me rest in green meadows,
he leads me beside peaceful streams.
He renews my strength."

His words flowed with the melody of the Windsong as though they were coming from the air around us.

"He guides me along right paths,
bringing honor to his name."

I laughed as he winked back at me, clearing some debris off the trail.

"Even when I walk through the darkest valley,
I will not be afraid,

for you are close beside me." [5]

He paused. "I'd like to learn that one," I told him.

"It's in the collection of scriptures Jesus packed in your bag." He nodded at the pack slung over my shoulder, and then pointed ahead as we walked forward. "Do you see that mountain, Tal? The next step in your path is over there."

I squinted to get a better look. The summit in the distance looked like a straight cliff.

Rohi stopped and whistled at a few wayward sheep, keeping a gentle eye on them until they returned to safety. He looked back at me. "Just listen for the Windsong, Tal."

"Oh, is that what you . . . we . . . call it? I mean—what is it?"

Rohi smiled. "It's the Spirit of God. His presence. The Spirit is always with you. Comforting. Guiding. Strengthening. He's quite the shepherd, if I do say so myself! His song is always there, but we don't always listen." He turned his head sharply toward his sheep. "Do we, children?"

The sheep continued to graze, oblivious to his playful scolding. He began to walk back the other way.

Words fumbled out of my mouth. "Hang on! Wait. Don't go yet. Is that all the explanation I get?"

Rohi felt safe. He felt sturdy. Being with him I had felt encouraged, calmed. Now I felt a little—abandoned.

Rohi walked back toward me and put his massive hands on my shoulders. "Remember, Tal, I am *always* with you. And I'm so proud of you. I've been waiting for you for a long time! The only instruction you need is to trust God. I think you've already had some experience with that." He nodded toward my Crest. His green eyes pierced through me. "It will give you light when you need it." He turned. "Now if you'll excuse me, I have to take

5. *Psalms 23:1-4a (NLT)*

these children to a fresh range." Just like that, he burst into song and marched off.

I stood still for what seemed like an eternity, listening to Rohi's singing slowly fading in the distance. *I am everywhere, and I take many forms.* I touched the Crest again, reminding myself that I was not alone.

Finally, when Rohi and his sheep had become dots on the horizon, I turned toward the rock face, holding up my hand to battle the glare of the sun. A good feeling surged through me. For some reason, I sensed that I was about to *do* something. Something meaningful. Important. All I'd done so far was leap into a river and eat a feast. There had been so much talking, questioning, listening, and thinking. And don't get me wrong—that had been wonderful. But surely now I was about to *go* somewhere and truly begin my adventure.

As I traveled toward the base of the mountain, I saw tents dotting the horizon. Soon I could hear the commotion and see people moving amongst the tents. It looked like a festival.

Campsites. Bonfires. Table spreads. People talking, laughing, and playing music. Where was I?

As I stood on the edge of the gathering, a tall, blonde woman approached me with an excited smile. "You're new here, aren't you?"

I smiled uncomfortably. "That obvious, huh?"

She laughed. "Well, you're coming from the forest and you're carrying a pack, so I took a guess. I'm Ingrid. Welcome!"

"Thanks! What is this place?" We began heading into the campsite, and I noticed that some of the dwellings looked more permanent than others. People must stay here awhile. Is this what Rohi meant when he said my next step was over here?

She looked around. "Well, I guess we don't really have a name for it. We should probably work on that. It's just the place you go after the Table." She continued to survey the assorted gatherings of people. "Hmmm, it's a field, so I guess you can call it the Field." She smiled. "Not very creative, I suppose."

I liked Ingrid. She seemed genuine. "What do we do in . . . the Field?"

Ingrid's face lit up. "We enjoy the Crest and being children of the King!"

I smiled. "That sounds pretty nice."

"Yes, and there's all sorts of ways to celebrate your Crest. There's a couple here who can do the most beautiful paintings of your Crest with your name around it. Also, there's a guy who can engrave your Crest in wood over the phrase *Child of the King*. There's a whole area of the Field that's designated for stuff like that. It's incredible. But I'm getting ahead of myself—I haven't even asked you your name!"

"Oh, I'm Tal. Rohi sent me over here."

She clapped. "Oh, Rohi is the best! I'm pretty sure he sent

all of us here!" She pointed toward a massive table that immediately reminded me of the Kingdom Table. "Come on, it's almost dinner time."

The dinner crowd was full of characters. I was thoroughly
entertained by Ingrid's nonstop stream of happy visitors and
friends. I wasn't the only person who enjoyed her warm, open
personality. Beyond her was a small group of friends discussing some cave I assumed must be up in the mountains. To my
left was a tribe of four. They were intensely strategizing how
to scale the rock face. One man was leaning forward intently,
explaining, "If I can hold my grip on the last ledge, I may be able
to pull myself up, even with no footing."

"If we had more faith I'm sure we could do it," his friend
replied fervently.

I watched them debate and discuss as they pointed to and
studied different parts of the mountain. I felt my blood stir. I
wanted to be strategizing right alongside them.

As the meal wrapped up, I approached the ringleader who
had been analyzing his climb and introduced myself.

"Great to meet you, Tal," he said with a warm smile and a
handshake. "I'm Kenric. I'll introduce you to the rest of the crew
in a bit."

"Sounds good. I overheard you all talking about scaling the
Rockface."

Kenric's eyes lit up as he looked toward it, now bathed in
moonlight. "Isn't it beautiful?"

"Rohi told me that's where the next part of the Path is."

He couldn't contain his excitement. "Yes!" He placed his
hand on my shoulder. "This is such an exciting part of the journey, Tal. We're learning how to tackle this thing. You know,

really do this life with dedication and passion. Do you want to come with us tomorrow?"

I looked toward it with a blend of excitement and apprehension. This guy and his friends were definitely the ones out there putting in the effort. "Yeah, but I'm not much of a climber . . . meaning, I've never climbed in my life."

Kenric chuckled. "It's okay, you'll get better as you go. You can even just watch tomorrow if you want. Give it some time and you'll be right there with us. I'll come get you in the morning."

That night Ingrid set me up with a comfortable place to sleep. As she turned to leave, I asked her a question. "Ingrid, have you tried to scale the mountain?"

She chuckled and shook her head. "No, Tal. Remember, the Crest is gifted to you, not earned. It's not achieved. We are invited to enjoy who we now are because of Jesus. The journey is over! You are loved, right here amongst new friends. Why should you have to scale an impossible mountain now? Kenric is great, but he takes this all a little too seriously. Jesus wants us to be happy, and the Field is a great place for that!"

I searched through my time with Jesus so far. Was that what he wanted? He certainly emphasized that the Crest was a gift. But didn't he also say that he had an adventure for me? And . . . I really wanted to see if I could scale the mountain. Was that bad?

"One more question," I said, "and then I promise I'll let you get some sleep. Did I hear some people talking about a cave?"

She looked toward the mountain. "Ah yes, the Cave. Lots of people talk about it. All I know is that it's dark and scary." She shuddered, and then laughed. "The Leap was scary enough! Why would Jesus want us to keep doing frightening things after that? The Field has everything we need, Tal. It's safe, it's full of friends, and we get to enjoy our new identity." She shrugged. "That's a pretty great life if you ask me!"

Ingrid smiled at me as I contemplated in silence. I felt a little confused.

"It was great to meet you, Tal. I'm so glad you're here."

I couldn't help but smile at her warmth. "Good night, Ingrid. Thanks for being so welcoming."

I must have fallen asleep almost immediately because it felt like the next moment I was being gently shaken awake by Kenric. My eyes slowly opened to his wide smile. "You ready, Tal?"

"Wow, this early?" I slowly sat up, trying to get my bearings. "Are you all against sleep or something?"

Kenric laughed. "All the climbers start early, Tal!"

I yawned as we quietly picked our way through the campsite in the gray predawn light, rubbing my face to try to wake up. Toward the edge of the Field, we passed a couple sitting on some boulders. The man, starting a campfire, looked over his shoulder and scowled. "Don't bother. You're only going to fail! No one has ever scaled that mountain."

Kenric put his arm around me and smiled. "Don't mind them, Tal. They may have grown weary in well doing, but we won't! Besides, I'm sure hundreds—maybe even thousands—of people have made it to the top. And no matter what, at least we're making progress, right?"

Approaching the base of the mountain, I saw the Cave. I had expected it to be higher up, tucked into the mountain. As I passed, I could have sworn I felt a whisper of . . . something.

"Do you want to just observe today, Tal?" Kenric's enthusiastic voice interrupted my thoughts. "Or do you want to try and trek with us?"

"Oh, no, you all go ahead! I don't want to slow you down. It'll be great just to see you in action!"

Kenric reached out his hand to shake mine. "Blessings on you, Tal! I'm so proud of you for choosing to be a Scaler."

"Thanks for bringing me along." I paused. "Kenric, one quick question before you take off. Why do so many people like Ingrid stay down in the Field?"

Kenric paused contemplatively. He seemed to be choosing his words carefully. "For some people, the Crest and the Field are as far as they think they need to go." He looked at me, his eyes full of both warmth and intensity. "But Tal, Jesus didn't invite us to just be believers—to sit back and enjoy. He invited us to be disciples, and that takes discipline. The Field and the Cave are both just people taking the easy way out. They don't take sin seriously, and so they don't take their growth seriously. We need to go out and tackle sin, just like we tackle this mountain." He started backing toward the mountain, clearly excited to get started. "Ingrid is a really nice woman." He smiled. "But Jesus wants more from us."

Just like that, he and his crew started moving up the mountain with skill and precision, the morning sun slowly rising up the Rockface.

I sat there for hours. The sun warmed my back as I watched in awe. Their skill, dedication, and courage was incredible. I could tell they'd been at this for a long time.

I could also feel myself itching to prove that I could do it too. That old voice hummed happily as I felt my motivation rise. *You can do that*, it whispered to me. *I bet you'll be way better than they expect. You'll show them how much you love Jesus, how seriously you take his call.*

The next morning I stood next to Kenric, looking up at the

cliff as he explained his method. He and his crew gave me some good climbing gloves and new shoes that would help me grip the toeholds better. I could feel the energy bubbling in my blood—it had been so long since I faced a real challenge! The Leap and the Table had been great, but I was ready for more. I was ready to show that I was a productive member of my new Jesus family.

Kenric showed me how to use my fingertips to find purchase on the Rockface and wedge my toes against the small cracks. Slowly, I began to climb. Only five feet off the ground my muscles began to shake as Kenric tried to guide me to my next handhold.

By midday my muscles had given up on me. But still, I was exhilarated. It felt so good to really push myself again, to throw all my effort in. I knew I could buckle down and train, and soon I'd be able to keep up. I had done it with architecture. Now I could focus that dedication and passion toward serving Jesus!

Ingrid tried to motion me over to their campfire that evening as I walked back, but I just waved and headed to my tent. I needed to train if I was going to start keeping up with Kenric and the other Scalers. And I was beginning to see his point. Ingrid and her friends—the Field Settlers—didn't take this whole following-Jesus thing seriously enough.

I began to fill my evenings with exercises to get stronger even though my muscles usually ached from the day's effort. But I would remind myself that with enough discipline and effort, I could catch up. I could get there. *Maybe even pass them,* the velvet voice murmured.

The progress was invigorating. One day about halfway up the Rockface, I pulled myself onto a ledge. I let my legs swing over the edge, looking out at the Field and toward the forest where I knew the Kingdom Table must be. A nice crisp breeze cooled my face. It was beautiful up here.

I thought back to Kenric's pep talk that morning. "Jesus did everything else for us," he had told us. "We need to do our part, too. So let's go out there and show Abba how dedicated we are."

A small frown creased my forehead as I remembered his words. They felt good. They felt . . . motivating. But something about them felt strange, too, like they were a half step off key. I thought back to Jesus' words from so long ago on the bluff. *"I did it all for you, Tal."*

My frown deepened. If he did it all for me, then . . . what was I doing up here? Was Ingrid right; we should just lounge in the Field and never try hard to grow? Or was Kenric right; we needed to show Jesus how serious we were?

You just want the easy way out, the minor key voice whispered. *Jesus wants you to make progress. He's probably disappointed that it's taken you this long—he had such high hopes for you.*

Unease spread through me as I turned back to look at the Rockface. The voice was right. I was barely halfway up—what was I doing taking a break? I pushed myself to my feet, determined to try harder. I pictured Jesus at the top, waiting for me. I wanted to show him how grateful I was for his sacrifice.

I didn't join the rest of the climbing crew for dinner that night. I ate on my own, just outside the lantern light cast by the large table. I felt like it was where I belonged. I didn't deserve to be with everyone else until I could catch up. Plus, in a way it felt better to nurse my frustration and self-judgment alone with stale bread to keep me company.

"You don't need to take care of anything before you come enjoy my Table. Your seat is waiting for you on your best days and on your worst days."

Abba's words came back to me like a gentle wind. I threw my stale bread in frustration, blocking their message out. I wished they felt true.

I became more frustrated than enthusiastic over the next few weeks. I would see Kenric and his friends ahead of me, and I would alternate between goading myself into trying harder and feeling hopeless that I would ever catch up. Some days I stayed in the Field with Ingrid and enjoyed company with friends, telling myself the Rockface was stupid and impossible. But by the next day I'd feel guilty and be back at it. I wanted to be one of the dedicated ones. I wanted to prove that I took Jesus seriously, that I was willing to put in the effort.

And finally, I had a breakthrough. For weeks I had been stuck, unable to make it past one of the upper ledges—until today.

Sweat trickled down my forehead as I braced my legs. My left hand had a good hold, and I could see where my right hand needed to go. *Come on, Tal. You can do this. Just try a little harder.* I reached, but my fingers could only scrabble at the edge. It was too far. *The others have done this. If you really had faith, if you were really trying, you'd get there too.* I tried to reposition my feet to give myself a few more inches, but it wasn't enough. I knew what I had to do. I just needed the courage for it.

I gathered my strength and pushed off, trying to grasp the rock before gravity found me.

Gravity won.

The rough surface was ripped from my hand and my body hit the ledge below with a groan. *What's wrong with you?* the velvet voice spat. *Why can't you do this?*

For five hours, I tried every route and combination possible to reach the next ledge. I'd get close—sometimes within inches—but I could never quite make it. Eventually I yelled in frustration, kicking the rock, which did nothing but add a hurt toe to my list of injuries. "I'm doing this for Jesus!" I screamed at the rock. And yet it felt like he was getting farther and farther away.

My last attempt was desperate. My fingers were already bloody from my other attempts. Bruises bloomed along my shins. I berated myself for my weakness and commanded my body to try harder. But gravity won again, my trembling muscles unable to help break my fall.

The wind was knocked out of me as my back hit the ledge— again. I hated the emotion that crawled up my throat.

Why, *why* would Rohi tell me to do this if it was just going to prove I was a failure? I couldn't bring myself to touch the Crest. If I were a child of the King, then I should be able to pull myself up past this ledge. Jesus did everything else. Why couldn't I meet him halfway?

The absence of the Windsong felt like a hole in my chest. Maybe it had left me. Maybe the Father was done guiding me. Maybe I hadn't done enough to stay close to him. I covered my face with my scraped hands.

The cruel voice in my head demanded that I try again, that I stop being so weak and useless. But I had nothing left to give. I cowed from the voice as it heaped shame on me, calling me all kinds of names. Defeated, I gingerly climbed back down to the ground and picked up my supplies. Maybe I'd just stay with Ingrid and stop trying. Clearly I couldn't hack it.

It felt like that day at the edge of Ican all over again. I couldn't keep up, I couldn't rise fast enough. That terrible feeling of disappointing Ricard and my dad and now *God* swept over me like a black tsunami.

I thought it would be different here.

I stared back at the mountain that had proved I wasn't enough and that I didn't belong with the true disciples.

As I lowered my eyes, they came to rest on the mouth of the Cave.

I stood there as dusk settled, staring at it, unable to look away. The last thing I wanted to do was enter a dark cavern with no inkling of what was inside. I was tired, hungry, and beaten. I wanted to go collapse in my tent and disappear from the world. And yet . . . I was still standing there.

I hesitated.

"Trust God," Rohi had told me. I thought about the Leap: how frightening it was and how I didn't know what would happen.

The memory of Jesus on that windswept bluff rose up in my mind. *"You can trust me, Tal."*

Unsure, I took a tiny step toward the Cave, thinking maybe I could see more of what was inside. A faint hum washed over me. Was that . . . what I thought it was?

I edged a little closer and could almost pick up the familiar melody. It grew, little by little, as my feet brought me to the edge of the darkness.

Even when I walk through the darkest valley,

I will not be afraid,

for you are close beside me.

Rohi had known, hadn't he?

I took a deep breath and took a step inside. If I had been nervous approaching the Cave, that was nothing to how I felt standing in its darkness. Panic. Fear. Dread closing in.

Then I saw it.

A small glimmer of light, glowing from my Crest like a distant sun.[6] I took another small step, and it grew brighter. The Windsong slowly built in a crescendo. Tears of relief welled up as I stumbled three more steps and fell to my bruised and

6. *Psalm 119:105*

battered knees. I didn't care. I tipped my head back, listening to the sweet music sweeping around me and watching the golden light radiate from my Crest.

The tears streamed down my cheeks as I let myself be enveloped in the light and the melody. Oh how I had missed this song!

I could hear Jesus' voice in the Windsong. *"I live within you, Tal. I never move, never distance, never turn away. There is nowhere you can go, in body or soul, that I will not be right with you.*[7] *Even when you* feel *far, you never are. I am always right here, inviting you to trust my love for you."*

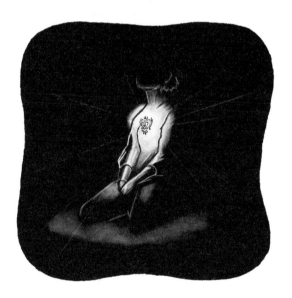

I don't know how long I stayed there, basking in the peace and joy of that beautiful song. But eventually, I slowly stood back up. The Crest gave me just enough light to see a step or

7. *Psalm 139:7-12; Romans 8:31-39; John 17:20-26*

two ahead of me. I remembered Rohi's words: *"He guides me along right paths, bringing honor to his name."*

The walk was fearful and wobbly at first. I truly didn't know what was ahead or where I was going. It was hard to trust the light of the Crest and the sound of the Windsong to guide me forward. But over time, my steps became more steady and firm, even as the light led me over boulders and across underwater streams, into narrow tunnels and across expansive, open caverns. The glow of the Crest and the melody of the Windsong kept me company. And slowly, almost imperceptibly, my fear transformed into joy, and my nervous steps became an adventure.

Guide Notes

What if all God wanted from you was to trust him?

In the upside down Kingdom of God, most things feel, well, upside down. Enemies are loved instead of hated. Suffering is a beautiful gift instead of a curse. Jesus died in defeat in order to bring life and victory. Up is down and down is up. The way of following Jesus is rarely the path we expect or the one we would design for ourselves.

When we entered this Kingdom, we left the world of I Can, of defining life for ourselves. We entered the Kingdom of He Can. We chose trust in God over trust in ourselves.

But trust can feel scary.

The Rockface [*of Striving*]

For some of us, trying to scale the Rockface is by far the most attractive course. We're natural Scalers. It keeps us in control. Trusting feels too passive, and it certainly doesn't feel like *doing*. We read our Bibles and memorize verses and serve in children's ministry and volunteer at a shelter and never miss church. We may white-knuckle our issues and gravitate toward communicators who tell us to shape up, take sin seriously, and prove that we're serious Christians. We are consistently disciplining ourselves to be better and do better. We'd probably say that we're sold out for Jesus; we want to show how much we love him and take his sacrifice seriously.

What might fear be saying to us here? The following questions can help us sort it out:

» Am I afraid of falling behind on my faith journey?
» Am I afraid of disappointing Jesus by not making "progress" fast enough?
» Am I afraid of losing my seat at the Table if I'm not passionate enough or dedicated enough?
» Am I afraid that others won't believe I'm enough unless I prove it?
» Am I afraid to trust that I truly cannot earn God's love or delight in me?
» Am I afraid that if I don't try to scale the Rockface I will give up on my faith?
» Am I afraid that God won't give me good things if I don't prove myself to him?

Fear will continue to poke and prod us to not trust what God has done for us. It thrives on our anxieties, pain, loneliness, self-judgment, and more. Fear wants to devastate our faith in the Crest and build up our faith in our own achievements. Fear does not want us to believe that our Crest will hold under any and all circumstances.[8]

But God will ask, "Why are you working so hard to do what only I can do?[9] There's only one thing that will make me pleased and proud of you—trusting me. I put this very simply in Hebrews 11:6, 'Without faith (trust) it is impossible to please me, God.' Don't let your old fears take you back to your old ways, when I have made you brand new."

So, when your fears inevitably prompt you to attempt the Rockface, listen for the voice of Jesus in the Windsong telling you, "Do not be afraid.[10] Remember the Table? I fully love and delight in you. Nothing you can do will earn or change that.[11] I have already scaled this Rockface *for* you; you don't need to even try it. Relax and enjoy!"

The Field [*of Passivity*]

Some of us aren't inclined toward the Rockface. We gravitate toward being a Field Settler. We believe that Jesus has saved us, redeemed us, and loves us right where we are. Why move from this spot? Those trying to scale the Rockface are a little too uptight—God wants us to do whatever makes us happy. Yes, he did a lot for us, but he doesn't want to be too involved in our daily lives.

In some areas we need his guidance and involvement, but there are some areas that we're pretty sure we can handle ourselves. We wouldn't call it control, necessarily . . . more like

8. *II Corinthians 5:17-21*
9. *Galatians 3:2-5*
10. *Luke 12:32*
11. *Romans 8:38-39*

division of labor. We'll let God lead some things, like our career, but we'll handle others, like our dating life. Sure, God cares about us reading our Bible and treating others well. But he probably doesn't care about our finances, our friendships, or our sex life. Right?

Besides, God seems to ask people to do pretty counter-cultural things, and that's scary. Like Ingrid said, "The Leap was scary enough. Why would God ask us to keep doing frightening things after that?"

Fear is a sneaky player. It dresses up in lots of different costumes. It drives some of us up the Rockface. But could fear be drawing you to the Field? Here are some questions to help:

» Am I afraid of being different from my friends that don't know Jesus?
» Am I afraid that if I let Jesus into some areas of my life, he might ask me to do something uncomfortable or even scary?
» Am I afraid that Jesus doesn't really have something important for me on this Path?
» Am I afraid to fail, so I don't even want to try?
» Am I afraid of the cost of following Jesus on this adventure?

Fellow traveler, Jesus has *so much* for you. The depths of his love and grace cannot be grasped.[12] The vastness of his plans for you cannot be captured. He cares about every part of you deeply and fully. That means he cares about your Sundays and your

12. *Ephesians 3:18-19*

random Tuesdays, your big life decisions and your stressed-out traffic mornings.[13] He's in for all of it.

Jesus is neither angry nor impatient as you learn to trust him with different pieces of your life. But in the quiet, you will hear his ever-present, gentle invitation:

» *Come and see* what plans I have for you.
» *Come and see* what happens when you trust me with more and more pieces of your life.
» *Come and see* how rich this life can be.[14]

The Cave [*of Trusting*]

The Bible tells us that we should keep following Jesus in the same way we first started—by trusting him:

And now, just as you accepted Christ Jesus as your Lord, you must continue to follow him. Let your roots grow down into him, and let your lives be built on him. Then your faith will grow strong in the truth you were taught, and you will overflow with thankfulness.

—COLOSSIANS 2:6-7 (NLT)

When we trust his love for us, our fears will be lessened.[15] Trusting God takes courage. It's challenging. It feels safer to stay in control. We can strive to do better and be better like

13. Psalm 139:16
14. John 1:39
15. I John 4:18

99

Kenric, or we can settle into the comfort of passivity like Ingrid. But...

> » Trusting God is the more challenging path.
> » Trust requires effort, and is never passive.
> » Trust requires yielding control instead of earning through striving.
> » Trusting is the way of Jesus.
> » Trusting is the only way we receive grace.

A huge part of learning to trust God is tuning your ear to hear the Windsong—the Holy Spirit. It's one of the most intimate and rewarding parts of the journey—developing your acute listening for that melody. When you hear it, pause. Something is up. Tal notices at the cave "a whisper of ... something." That is how the gentle wind of the Spirit works.[16] We rarely have all the details when we begin to hear or feel the Spirit. He provides those details as needed, and they are often only understood with hindsight. This life of trust is lived forwards, but understood backwards.

Remember when you got your first car? Whether you loved the way it looked or felt embarrassed being seen in it, did you notice how you kept seeing the same make and model all over the place? You had possibly never even thought about that type of car when you passed it before. Now you saw it everywhere you looked!

That's how it works with the Holy Spirit. Over time as you lean in, you will sense him, hear him, and feel him more. He will be with you and show up around you. You will notice him in more places.

16. John 3:8; Romans 8:26-27

He will never whisper anything to you that contradicts Jesus. So if you think something awful about yourself, that's *not* him. The Windsong is God with us, comforting us, and guiding us.[17] And God's heart toward us is *always* good.[18]

For a while, Tal struggled to hear the Windsong, and thought that this must mean God was far away. This will not be the last time Tal (or any of us) feels this way. But the incredible, freeing truth is that even when we struggle to hear or feel God's nearness, he is still fully present within us. We never need to get "back to God" who is "over there." He is always with us! We only need to trust this truth, even when our feelings struggle to take it in. If you find yourself in such a season, breathe. Relax. He is with you, even if you do not sense him. It can be helpful in this place to ask, "In what area might Jesus be inviting me to trust right now?"

When you do hear the Windsong and sense that God is inviting you into the Cave where you can't see what's next, take a step. Surprise! The Crest begins to glow. Jesus himself is the Light, and he has embedded his constant light in you.[19] The light is always there. The flame never goes out. The bitter wind or pressing dark can never extinguish it.[20] Your Crest is *always* ready to shine anywhere. But the Crest lights up brightest when you cannot see what's next, when you journey into the darkness, when you take the next step.

---

17. John 14:16; John 16:12-15; Romans 8:5-6
18. Romans 8:28-31
19. I Thessalonians 5:4-6; Philippians 2:15
20. John 1:5

How do I know where I'm living?

We move between the Field, Rockface, and Cave often, and sometimes we are living in different places in different areas of our lives. One helpful question to reflect on is, "What is my effort focused on?" In the Field, our effort is focused on *staying comfortable.* At the Rockface, our effort is focused on *moving forward through our own willpower.* In the Cave, our effort is focused on *yielding to (trusting) Jesus' love and leading in our lives.* Remember: grace is not opposed to effort, grace is opposed to earning.

Another area we see these three play out is in how we're viewing our identity.

» In the Field, we believe, "My new identity is a nice add-on to my life, but it doesn't really affect my decisions. I might be a sinner, but that's okay, God loves me anyway."

» At the Rockface, we believe, "My new identity wiped the slate clean, but now I need to work hard to become a new person. I'm a sinner, striving to become a saint."

» In the Cave, we believe, "My new identity fundamentally changed me forever and is real and complete. The rest of my life is letting Jesus teach me how to live out of what is now true. I'm a saint, who still sins."

Trust does not nullify fear. Or delete doubts. Or eliminate flinches.

We took the leap into the unknown by trusting Jesus with our whole selves. We never graduate from learning this important truth. The rest of our lives are spent learning to trust him in new places along the Path.

When you (inevitably) get stopped in your tracks along the Path, some of the best advice comes from these famous Old Testament verses, Proverbs 3:5-6:

> *Trust in the Lord with all your heart. Do not lean on your own understanding, but in all your ways trust him, and he will make your paths straight.*

Selah

These choices do not arrive once and then depart. We circle them daily, moment by moment. Will we try to earn our worth, or abdicate our role? Will we strive to do it ourselves, or avoid the cost of engagement?

. . . or will we trust?

Will we venture into that mysterious dark that is full of God-knows-what? Full of perhaps joy and adventure but perhaps pain and heartbreak, too?

He sees you hovering, hoping to step, fearing to fall. Trying to trust the One who can see in the dark. He is most gentle with you.

Where does he invite you to travel more deeply?

THE WOUND

Fear will cause you to view things in such a twisted manner that you'll lose all healthy sense of perspective. Then you will doubt what you should trust, and trust what you should doubt.

—LISA BEVERE

We have an ancient and cunning enemy who is bent on weaponizing our pain.

It begins early. A callous word, a withheld gaze, a cruel violation. He finds a way in for each of us—the first cut in what will become a festering wound. To ensure this wound doesn't heal, he wraps it in darkness, convincing us that it must never see light or healing or love. He feeds on the wound, using our pain to slice others and continue the cycle.

Dear traveler, your Healer sees you limping and oozing. And he asks most gently,

"Do you want to be healed?"[1]

---

1. John 5:6

I stood at the top of a ridge, looking out over the land ahead. Rolling hills stretched west, and to the north a mountain range rose like the spine of a great beast. The clatter of pans and the strike of a match sounded behind me. The rest of the group was making camp.

This was my favorite time of day. The sun sank down and threw a last-minute blanket of color over the world. The Windsong wrapped around me, bringing the scent of green and growing things.

I turned back to the group, smiling at the familiar sense of amazement. Life on this side of the Cave was better than I could have dreamed. It was adventurous, even dangerous, and wonderful. I had learned more about Jesus and myself than I

thought possible. As I walked up to the group, Gia threw me a log. She knew I loved building the fire each night.

I first met Gia and Aran in the Cave, fellow travelers trying to learn how to trust Jesus in the dark. I was trying to cross a deep ravine but couldn't quite see the other side. Just then, Gia and Aran had shown up, and their Crests threw out the extra light I needed to see the way. We had gathered more people as we traveled, finding other followers to journey beside. Together we had faced challenges that we could never have navigated alone.[2]

I smiled as I rearranged the logs of the fire, remembering when we had practically dragged Gia through a tight tunnel. Her claustrophobia had set in, so she shut her eyes and we carried her through.

"Yeah, my mom used to have these big anger explosions," Gia was telling Aran as I sat down. "Like, the littlest thing would set her off, and sometimes it would seem so out of nowhere. So I was always watching her, trying to figure out what mood she was in so I wouldn't step on a landmine. I think I still kind of do that subconsciously with other people—I'm constantly trying to read them."

"I get that," I muttered.

"Yeah?" Gia offered.

"Yeah." I nodded, staring at the fire. They were both silent, inviting me to continue if I wanted to. "I mean, I know that feeling of trying to figure out how to make a parent happy." I shrugged. "My dad. I mean, he wasn't angry. It was more like, I don't know, I wasn't worth his attention unless I was doing something really impressive."

I readjusted the logs, wanting to keep the conversation light.

2. I Corinthians 12:12-26

"That sucks, Tal," Aran said simply.

"Eh, it's not a big deal," I lied. "Made me pretty cutthroat when it came to competition, though." I forced a laugh.

"Is that so?" Aran smiled and tossed me an apple. "What'd that get you?"

"Hmm, let's see," I took a bite of the apple. I counted on my fingers, "Third Key, panic attacks, and, that's right—crushing loneliness." I genuinely laughed, and Gia and Aran chuckled with me. "That's how I came to meet Jesus."

"I think we all have similar stories of what led us to Jesus," Aran smiled a little sadly. "Third Key, though. Wow. That's . . . really impressive."

"Yeah, maybe don't tell anyone that," I said quickly, glancing around the fire. "It's not something I'm exactly proud of. Or want widely known."

"Fair enough," Gia said. I got up to get another log for the fire.

We began heading north the next day toward those foreboding mountains. Aran, who had become the de facto leader of our group, had heard there was a settlement of other followers that way.

The terrain got tougher, rockier. Conversation became more stilted along the road as we all struggled to keep our breath. I kept replaying my conversation with Gia and Aran, worrying that I had said too much. I didn't want them to see me as weak or with "issues." I felt embarrassed for telling them I got Third Key. *Why even bring that up? Were you trying to brag? Draw attention to yourself? And why are you so awkward when you're trying to make conversation? It's so easy for everyone else.*

We made it to the base of the mountain range, and the climb was steep as we wound our way upward. I was struggling to keep up with the pace, trying to keep my ragged breath unnoticed. I had slowly fallen to the very back of the line. I tried to ignore the cruel voice in my head hissing to *hurry up. Push harder. Don't be the weak link.*

Distracted by the increasing gap between me and the next person, my foot slipped off a large boulder. A jagged edge ripped into the side of my calf, drawing an involuntary gasp as I stumbled.

My first instinct was to look ahead. Had anyone heard me? Had anyone noticed? I was relieved to see no heads turning my direction.

How could I have been so stupid? I inspected the cut. It was deep, blood already dripping down. Thinking quickly, I pulled out a shirt from my pack and wrapped it tightly around the cut, glancing up every few seconds to make sure no one had noticed my mistake.

I tied the shirt off, grunting slightly at the pressure. Then I pulled some loose pants out of my bag and pulled them over my shorts to hide the makeshift bandage.

I clenched my teeth as I put weight on my leg. The group was getting farther ahead, so I pulled on my pack and pushed onward, trying to ignore the shooting pain.

By the time I had caught up to the group, it was already time to break for the night.

"We wondered where you'd gotten off to!" Gia called as I forced myself not to limp.

I moved toward the fire to help, but Gia had already built it. "Oh, I took care of that," she said as she pulled out some of the spices from her food pack. "I thought you might want a break."

As we ate dinner that night, I was quiet. My anxiety was escalating along with the pain. I felt on the outside of every conversation, and I worried about why Gia thought I needed a break. The discussion turned to where we were going the next day, and my lungs felt tight. Could I keep up tomorrow?

I nodded my goodnights an hour later and slipped into my tent, making sure the flaps were closed tight. My leg felt like it had its own heartbeat. Slowly, I peeled off the blood-soaked shirt.

The wound looked even worse than it had before. I tried pouring some of my water on it, and had to bite my fist to keep from screaming. I wrapped the shirt back around it, wondering if I shouldn't have looked at all.

Everyone was energetic and excited the next morning, but I had barely slept, my leg throbbing and aching through the night.

"Everything okay?" Aran asked me, clapping a hand to my shoulder. "You don't look so great."

"Oh, I'm fine," I said, waving my hand. "Just found some good rocks to sleep on last night, that's all."

He laughed. "Well, gotta keep up today!" He headed off to

shoulder his bag as my heart sank. He had noticed that I was getting slower.

It was worse—so much worse—that day. I fell farther and farther behind. I barely made it to the lunch break in time to sit down. Everyone else had already finished their food.

"You sure you're alright, Tal?" Gia asked, concern lining her face.

"Totally," I responded. I forced my voice to sound chipper.

"Good thing you've got that cutthroat nature, huh?" Aran winked at me.

I forced a laugh, but I was stunned. *I can't believe he just threw that in my face.* But my shock was quickly replaced with anger. *This is why you don't share stuff with people. This is why you keep it hidden. They'll just use it against you.*

I excused myself a few minutes later. Stepping behind a large boulder, I pulled my pant leg up to check my self-made bandage. I could see the blood was oozing through it already.

I heard a gasp behind me. "Oh my gosh, Tal, what's wrong with your leg?!" Gia's eyes were wide and—disgusted?

Immediately I dropped my pant leg back down, shame washing over me. I could feel my cheeks heating. "Nothing," I said, a little too quickly. "It's nothing. I'm fine."

She looked unsure. "But don't you need—"

"I'm fine, Gia," I forced a chuckle to convince her. "I'm just clumsy, that's all. And out of shape. I can't keep up with the hiking champs like you!"

"Okay," she said slowly. "Well, I was just going to let you know that we're packing up."

"Great," I replied confidently, "I'll be ready."

She turned back to the group. I wasn't sure if that was what I wanted or not.

By mid-afternoon I knew I couldn't keep going. I just stood there on the steep trail, the sounds of the group having faded away at least an hour before. Aran's "cutthroat" comment seemed to have drained the last energy from me. And now that Gia had seen my wound, I just wanted to fade away. Disappear.

I felt my throat tighten. Anger and desperation threatened to overtake me. I heard that velvet voice whisper, *You can't hack it. You're not good enough to keep up. You've been found out.*

A strong wind started to blow, and I looked up to find angry clouds slowly making their way toward me. *Of course.* I needed to find shelter.

The dark clouds rolled in fast, and before I had gone very far, large drops began to pepper my face. As I came around a corner, I took a step too close to the edge, and, too late, I felt the earth give way.

I had barely a moment to feel the spike of fear before I was rolling and flailing. I felt the wound tear open again as the makeshift bandage ripped off, and felt the sharp sting as my palms tried to grab onto anything solid.

I hit an embankment with a thud and stopped as abruptly as I had started. My whole body hurt now. I looked up the slope, but there was no way I could scale back up in my condition. The sky was nearly black as the rain picked up and drops fell faster on my upturned face.

Hopelessness closed on my chest like a fist. Alone. All alone.

See? You're broken. You thought you could fake it, but I know who you really are, the velvet voice whispered. I could practically hear the smile in its voice. It was right. I had tried. But in the end, I was the same broken person as before. Unseen. Unloved.

Who would love someone like you?

I pressed my hand to my chest like it would ease the terrible weight sitting there.

And the world went black.

∞

My eyelids were still closed when I noticed the flicker of flames.

I cracked my eyes open. I was in a shallow cave. The light of the flames danced against the curved wall.

Slowly my senses came back. I could feel a heavy blanket on my legs. A dark-haired woman was tending the fire. She looked over as though she could sense my eyes had opened.

"You're awake," she said gently, walking over to me. I could hear the patter of rain outside.

I grunted, pushing myself up to a sitting position.

She sat on the edge of the cot. "My name is Rapha."[3] Her eyes were warm with decades of tears and laughter etched into her face.

"Nice to meet you, Rapha," I grunted the last word as my calf gave a painful twitch.

She began lifting the blanket to see what was wrong.

"Don't," I managed to gasp. I didn't want her to look at it. *I didn't want to look at it.*

Don't let her see, the voice hissed. *She'll be disgusted.*

Rapha paused with her hand still on the edge of the blanket.

"Tal," she said gently, and there was such tenderness in her voice that I felt my throat tighten. She knew my name, and I didn't care how.

"Please," I croaked. "Please don't look at it."

3. *Exodus 15:26*

She reached out and cupped my face in her weathered hands. "But I want to heal you, Tal.[4] And I can't heal you if you don't let me see the wound. I know that the Shamesong is telling you to hide. But that is not the voice of God."

"I failed," I choked out. "I couldn't keep up. There's something wrong with me."

"Oh, child." She pulled me into a hug. "Everyone fails, and falls, and gets hurt. Everyone needs healing. That's why I'm here."

I longed for her comfort, but part of me reeled from her closeness, wanting to push her away. I pulled back, quickly wiping my face. "No one else in my group fell back or got hurt."

"You don't know that," she said with a soft smile. "And you don't know what has happened before you met them or what

4. *Psalm 147:3*

116

will happen later. But I promise you, everyone gets hurt and needs my healing."[5]

As she smiled, I noticed that the Windsong was humming through the cave in the background of our conversation. When had I stopped hearing it?

"You called it the Shamesong," I said quietly.

"Yes," she replied. Sadness flickered in her eyes. "The Shamesong will continue to speak to you, Tal. It whispers to everyone, trying to draw them back to Ican, trying to convince them that they aren't really who Jesus says they are, that Jesus didn't really free them from the curse. The one who sings it is old, persuasive, and can be remarkably subtle.[6] He's very talented, and he will always try to get you to sing his song instead of the melody of God."

I traced the velvet voice back through my life and remembered its minor key as a near-constant refrain in the back of my mind.

Rapha continued, "But the Shamesong is no match for the gracesong, or the Windsong as you call it."[7] Her smile deepened. "It will outsing shame in the end. You just have to listen for its melody."

"But the Shamesong is right," I said after a few moments, fiddling with the edge of the blanket. "I . . . I wasn't enough. I've never been enough. Not with Aran and Gia. Not with Ricard. Not with my . . . " I swallowed, unable to finish. I took a shaky breath. "I feel like, at the core, it's right. I'm not enough."

Rapha shook her head, "Tal, do you remember being out on that bluff with Jesus before you took the Leap?"

5. Romans 3:23; Revelation 21:4

6. John 8:44; I Peter 5:8

7. Ephesians 6:11-18

I nodded.

"What was he trying to tell you?"

I thought back to what felt like another lifetime. "That . . . that he had done everything for me. That he would do it again . . . just for me. That I could trust him."

"And what about back at the Table with Abba? What was he wanting to teach you?"

I took a deep breath as I thought. "That I now belonged to him, and that he was my Father. That I was new." I placed my fingers gingerly on the Crest. "That Jesus now lived inside me." My brow furrowed.

Rapha nodded. "Jesus felt that you were worth his very life, Tal.[8] That's true when you feel it and when you don't. When you act like it and when you don't. Shame tries to tell you that you are who you *were*, and that at the end of the day you're still a grubby sinner. But grace tells you that at the end of the day, you are a beloved, holy saint—cherished, pursued, delighted-in. God's word has the final say, not shame. Jesus says that you are enough. Your journey is learning to trust that. Remember, Jesus didn't just die for your sins. He died for your shame, too."

I took a few more deep breaths, steadying myself. Rapha continued to smile at me, and I knew what she was waiting for.

Shame begged for me to hide. But the Windsong's melody was achingly beautiful, breaking my heart and breaking it open at the same time.

"Okay," I finally said as the flames threw shadows on the cave walls. "Okay."

Slowly, I peeled the blanket back. The wound looked even worse than I thought it would. The edges had turned white and

8. *John 3:16*

there was a faint odor coming from it. I looked up at Rapha, expecting to see my disgust mirrored on her face.

But instead, she was looking at the wound with deep, fathomless compassion. "Oh, Tal." She put her hand on my shoulder. "This must be so painful. And you've tried to keep hiking? That must have been exhausting." She shook her head slowly. "I'm so sorry you've been carrying this."

My heart clenched at the empathy in her voice.

"Just exposing it to oxygen like this helps,"[9] she told me. "I'll need to clean it out, put some ointment on it, and bind it to start with. Why don't you tell me what happened?"

As she softly set about cleaning the wound, I began to tell her my story. I told her first about slipping on the boulder and trying to hide it. There were a few sharp breaths as she carefully applied the cleaning solution, the wound stinging. But her movements were endlessly gentle, precise, and sure. She whispered quiet murmurs of comfort as she worked.[10]

I began telling her about my dad. How I never felt enough for him or his attention. How it still made my heart sink to even think about it. How I had tried to ignore that pain for the last few years. Rapha listened and nodded, offering compassion and her steady presence as I allowed some of the pain to release. Gently she began offering me truths of who my true Father was, how he saw me, how he paid endless attention to me. How he had been present with me in all those moments I felt unseen and unloved.[11]

I ached. And grieved. And hoped.

And I began to heal.

9. *I John 1:7*
10. *II Corinthians 1:3-5*
11. *Hosea 11:3-4; Psalm 139*

Guide Notes

What if your deepest wound is where God longs to bring your deepest healing?

If you don't address the wounds of your past, you continue to bleed.

—TINA TURNER

Each of us carry wounds.

From as early as we can remember—or earlier—each of us have absorbed injuries and abuses. No one escapes wrongs and hurts in this broken world. All of us are wounded.

And, all of us are wounders.[12]

Many of us have tried various ways to deny our wounds. Or if not deny, at least cope around them, doing our best to make life work in spite of them. This is why many of us continue to

12. *Romans 3:23*

bleed internally even after we have bandaged up our external wounds. Someone apologizes for the harsh word they spoke or the time they forgot your lunch date. This can put a bandage on, but inside we're still oozing. And out of that wounding, we slice open others in our lives, spreading the infection.

Pause for a moment. Can you identify your deeper wounds? Most of us cannot do so on our own. We need others to help us. We have spent so long avoiding, denying, or numbing our wounds that the road has become tangled and obscured. We have suffered:

Rejection, abandonment, humiliation and betrayal.
Injustice, setbacks, failure, and disappointment.
Frustration, regret, sorrow, and losses.
Being bullied, left out, unseen, and unheard.

Sadly, there are hundreds of options from which to choose. Our broken world continues to break our hearts.

One of the common avoidance strategies to manage our wounds is to stoically say, "It is what it is." Loosely translated, "Hard stuff happens in life, but I live above it." That's shame saying, "Don't stoop down to being hurt by this. You're better than that. Walk away. Let it go. Get on with your life."

Another common ducking strategy is, "Time heals all wounds." When we say this we think we can simply ignore a wound and assume time will take care of it. But this is another myth. Unresolved wounds don't heal themselves—they are simply buried alive. And when we bury things alive, they eventually re-emerge as zombies: unrecognizable and destructive forces in our internal worlds.

Shame: The Song of the Enemy

So why don't wounds heal on their own? Why can't our wounds be reduced to, "It is what it is," or "Time heals all wounds"?

Something deeper than the wound itself is at work. There's a superficial wound (what happened to us), and there's a deeper, more chronic wound (what it means to us and what we think it says about us). Did you notice how Tal's *reaction* to the wound was far more serious than the wound itself, leading to much more serious consequences?[13] Shame does that. Shame relentlessly causes us to take more damaging missteps than whatever created the first cut.

Shame is the deeply embedded voice that causes us to ask, "Am I enough?"

It's not even asking, "Did I do wrong?" (guilt) but instead, "Is there something wrong *with me*?" (shame).

This question is an identity statement. Shame doesn't just want to get at our behaviors. Those are small fish. It wants to get at our very core, who we believe we are. This will then affect every area of our lives.

This is why we never graduate from learning to trust God with *who we are*. Have you noticed how often Tal needs to return to this truth? We return to the Kingdom Table again and again, letting God remind us what our Crest means. Shame will constantly invite us to doubt this.

This is an old song. It all started when the enemy convinced Adam and Eve to doubt God's goodness. When they made their

13. II Samuel 11. See how David's reaction to his initial sin created even more serious consequences.

catastrophic choice to follow the voice of shame, they suddenly realized something was wrong with them. And like Tal, they tried to hide. This is the first instance of fear and hiding we know of in history.[14] A paragraph earlier Adam and Eve were naked and felt no shame.[15] Now, suddenly, they have gone into hiding out of fear *because* they are naked and ashamed. What happened?

The evil voice of shame came looking for them, entering and overpowering their lives. Shame is always ready to voice an intruding opinion about your defectiveness or deficiency. It's always ready to disrupt, divide, and destroy your relationships.

The goal of this voice is to:

» Prevent you from trusting who you are.
» Prevent you from letting others love you.
» Limit your ability to love others.

As Curt Thompson writes in his book *The Soul of Shame*, "In the biblical narrative when we experience shame, we are not simply encountering one of an array of possible emotions; rather we are engaging evil in its most fundamental mode of operation." The emotion that shame stirs up in us remains the central reason our wounds do not heal over time. Shame is perfectly happy with someone saying, "It is what it is." As shame is flowering into a hundred different symptoms, it also knows we will hardly recognize they all have their root in one evil voice—the enemy, the First Wounder.

14. *Genesis 3:1-7*
15. *Genesis 2:25*

Listening for God's Song

For the Lord your God is living among you. He is a mighty savior. He will take delight in you with gladness. With his love, he will calm all your fears. He will rejoice over you with joyful songs.

—ZEPHANIAH 3:17 (NLT)

Shame is tricky. One day it will whisper barely-audible thoughts in your mind, and the next it'll blare messages at front-row concert volume. With its many twists and turns, shame is outrageously complex. There's no simple formula for responding to it. There are, however, a few things you can remember when you notice those off-key Shamesong notes to help you turn your ear back to God's song of healing.

1. Remember Who God Is

If the starting place in addressing your wounds is recognizing the presence of the First Wounder, the ending place must always be recognizing the Wounded Healer. Jesus is the only God who bears the scars of evil. Jesus took *our* wounds, sin, and shame on himself.[16]

Time doesn't heal all wounds. Jesus does.

Astonishingly, it is *by* his wounds we can be healed.[17] Jesus came to heal not only sin and pain, but also our shame.

16. *II Corinthians 5:21*
17. *Isaiah 53:5; I Peter 2:24*

He came to heal the deeper wound, which is the fundamental fracture in our hearts. One of the ways he does this is by helping us see how loved we are by his Father. Jesus knew exactly what God the Father was like.[18] And when he explains it to his disciples, he tells a story about a wild child son who essentially tells his dad that he wishes he were dead, takes his money, leaves, and spends the last dime partying. The son realizes he has screwed up and decides to go beg for his dad to let him just be a servant in his house. Talk about some shame.

How would you expect God to respond? Cross his arms? Make you prove how sorry you were? Tell you he *has* to love you because he's God, but he doesn't like you much right now? That is your shame talking to you, friend. Instead, Jesus tells us:

"... and while he was still a long way off, his father saw him coming. Filled with love and compassion, he ran to his son, embraced him, and kissed him."[19]

Jesus reminds us that even in our deepest shame, this is what God is like—an open-armed father, running out to welcome his child home.

2. Remember Who You Are

When you recognize the sultry tone of the Shamesong—whether playing delicately or deafeningly in your head—you can either sing along, or you can let the Wounded Healer change the station, telling you . . .

18. Matthew 11:27
19. Luke 15:20 (NLT)

» "When shame tells you that you are unlovable, I will remind you that you are loved to the end of time itself. Your very nature is an eternally Loved One."[20]

» "When shame tells you that you are not enough, I will remind you that you are enough for me. I am within you, fueling and powering you. Even your weaknesses are precious to me because that is where you let me love you."[21]

» "When shame tells you that your true self is hideous, I will take your face in my hands and tell you that I crafted every piece and aspect of who you are, and I find my work stunning and flawless."[22]

» "When shame tells you that you are alone, I will shout from the mountaintops that I AM WITH YOU. You are never alone, child. There is no moment you will live or breathe that I am not fully with and within you."[23]

When shame kicks up, it is a great time to return to the Kingdom Table. Drink deeply and fill your belly with his good food. Breathe in the grace that drenches his presence and breathe out the lies that burden you. Let Abba remind you that you are chosen, holy, dearly loved, righteous, and his kid.

20. *Jeremiah 31:3; Romans 8:38-39*
21. *II Corinthians 12:9; Philippians 4:13*
22. *Psalms 139:14; Ephesians 2:10*
23. *Deuteronomy 31:6; Matthew 28:20*

3. Remember What You Were Made For

You are created for deep connection with others—it's in your DNA (more about that in the next chapter). This is also the first place that shame attacks.

When we see ourselves through the lens of shame like Adam and Eve, it leads to hiding. Shame tells us, "If they really knew you, they wouldn't love you." When we believe this, we end up feeling alone and disconnected, even if we've got lots of people in our lives. We don't feel safe to be truly known. It's the perfect recipe to keep triggering this cycle of hurt, shame, and hiddenness.

On the other hand, when we see ourselves as loved, chosen sons and daughters of the King, we can rest in a secure identity. This security allows us to be vulnerable because we know at the end of the day that we are loved and we belong even in the midst of all our mess ups and flaws. We can then let others see our wounds, which allows us to be known and loved—exactly what we're longing for!

Good news: Wounds are not fatal.

Better news: Healing from wounds can lead you into a more thriving future than you ever imagined. As Henri Nouwen writes in his book *The Wounded Healer*, "As followers of Jesus we can also allow our wounds to bring healing to others." We are wounded in relationships. We are also healed in relationships.[24] It's good to heal with God like Tal is. But God then calls us to heal with others . . . as Tal will.

---

24. *Mark 2:3-5*

∽

The next morning I awoke to Rapha packing up her supplies and my pack.

"Are you leaving?" I asked as I sat up. My leg felt much better already, but I didn't know if I was up for a long walk quite yet.

"*We* are leaving," she smiled. "It's time for you to rejoin the group. I will use them to continue healing your wounds."

Fear spiked through me. "What? No. No, I don't want them to know about this. Why can't you just take care of it?"

She smiled knowingly. "I understand. It feels easier to just tend it quietly between you and me. But that's not what you're made for, Tal. God made you to need the hands, feet, and words of others, and for them to need yours. In fact, that's most often how God works. It can be tempting to just have God tend our wounds, but then you miss out on some of the true beauty and transformation of healing."

She must have seen the uneasiness on my face. She knelt down next to the cot. "You are brave, Tal. This is a hard step, I know. But I promise, just like the Cave, the beauty that is possible on the other side is so worth it."

She held my eyes, and with a deep breath I finally nodded.

"Then let's go." She held out her hand as I stood up, and it was like I was right back on that bluff with Jesus, waiting to take the Leap. *I take many forms,* Abba had told me. Indeed.

I took her hand. For the first time I noticed a tunnel leading deeper into the mountain.

"Another Cave?"

"Another chance to trust even when you aren't sure what's ahead," she explained with a smile.

We took a step, and suddenly we were up on an outcropping with a gentle wind swirling around us.

"What? How—where did we—" I looked around, and she just laughed, the sound like a splashing river.

The group was leaning against a ledge a little ways down the trail, probably taking a lunch break. My heart clenched painfully. I tried to ignore the Shamesong clamoring for my attention as Rapha called out to them.

"Tal!" Aran yelled. He leapt up and ran over, pulling me into a tight hug. "Oh my gosh, I'm so glad you're back. We were so worried. Where were you?"

"Um," I started uncomfortably, looking around at the faces as everyone made their way over. "Well," I took a deep breath, glancing at Rapha. "I got . . . hurt. And I couldn't keep up or keep going. I didn't want anyone to know." I looked at Rapha again, and she nodded encouragingly. "I'm still on the mend. So I'll need some help as we go. And I might need to go a little slower. I'm sorry."

Quiet fell in the group. Aran sighed and sat down.

My heart started to pound painfully. The tunnel vision started.

"Tal . . . " he paused. And then without another word, he pulled up the side of his shirt.

It looked like he had scraped four square inches of skin clean off the side of his torso. There were sections that had tried to scab, but then cracked and bled.

"It happened about a week ago," he said heavily. "I've been hurting so much, but I was the leader, you know? I didn't—I *couldn't*—let you all down. But I can't carry my supplies the same way. And I know I hurt you with that stupid cutthroat comment," he shook his head again. "I was in my own head, so worried about making sure *I* kept up, that it just spilled over. I'm sorry, Tal. I was hurting so I hurt you. And I hate admitting it, but I need help, too."

I crouched down in front of him.

"Hey, Rapha showed me how to clean these wounds," I said gently. "I can help."

Selah

Listen. Do you hear it? Rasping on the edges? Slithering
through the familiar waters? Wrapping quietly
around your heart?

We hum along, preferring the tune we know. The tune
we have been taught. Even as it drags its claws along
our minds, we sing the oozing harmony. We let it fill us,
memorizing its notes, its rises and falls.
We sing the cruel melody back to ourselves.

But listen. Do you hear it, rising, gathering, shining?
There is another song. Deeper than the foundations
of the earth, stronger than the universe itself, more
beautiful than human words will ever be able to grasp.

It is the eternal song of love,
sung through the ages and the cosmos and your
very soul.

Which melody will you sing?

THE GATHERING

They reminded me that Christianity isn't meant to simply be believed; it's meant to be lived, shared, eaten, spoken, and enacted in the presence of other people. They reminded me that, try as I may, I can't be a Christian on my own. I need a community.

—RACHEL HELD EVANS

We may say that we have grown up and matured. We are above such a silly need as friendship or community. Our lives consist of layers, levels, and hidden dead ends to keep us from the pleasure and pain of being known and loved. Too many hurts. Too many breaches of the wall. So the wall grows thicker and the brambles more wild until we are left lonely and "safe" in our tower.

But hidden deep in that fortress of our hearts is the wild wonder of a child, longing to run and play with a pack of sure-footed friends. Dear traveler, throw open your bolted door once again to the wide open spaces of grace and the brave, glorious friendships waiting outside.

The cool stone felt good on my forehead.

I let my eyes close. It had been a long day. A good day, but a long day.

Our group found the settlement Aran had heard of months ago. The Gathering, as it was called, was a beautiful village nestled in the hills. Unlike Ican, where the Grand Hall sat high above the common people, the Gathering was spread out with vibrant pockets of structures and people. We had all settled in, finding our way and the kind of community we had only dreamed of.

I made myself sit up, noticing how stiff I was. Gia was right—I'd been pushing myself too hard recently. She was good at noticing when I was starting to slide back toward striving to earn my identity instead of enjoying it. Or, as she would say, I was "working *for* my identity instead of *from* my identity." She would remind me that I didn't have to try harder to become loved. That the real me was worthy of it right now.

I looked around the cavernous room I sat in. It looked like a mess with hewn rock in one corner and stacked lumber in another. Everything was covered in a fine layer of dust.

I smiled.

When we first arrived at the Gathering I had avoided building, trying my hand at other work. It had taken several brave conversations with Aran for me to even consider using my architecture talent in Jesus' Kingdom. I was nervous that I would revert to who I used to be in Ican, that I wouldn't be any good anymore, or that people would look at me differently for stepping out. But Aran and Gia were both firm supports. Tentatively, I began offering to help on a few town projects. To my delight—and occasional alarm—others connected with my ideas. They actually began asking for my thoughts and inviting me into larger initiatives.

It felt like some part of me was coming back alive, but in a totally different way. Unlike in Ican, where my talent was *the thing* people recognized me for, the Gathering appreciated it as one part of the whole. They cared about *all* parts of me as a full person.

I had developed some deep, meaningful friendships in this place. I trusted them with the real me, with my real stuff, and they trusted me too. I had never felt so known and loved.

I pushed myself up from the table and walked over to the arched opening where a window would one day go. The golden light of dusk was settling over the village, bouncing off a few of the roofs. Others might see a mess, but I saw the possibility of what was being built. One day this would be the new School Hall, a place for the children in the Gathering to learn and play and discover. It was the first project where I was chief architect, and I felt so . . . fulfilled.

I sighed, content.

I have so much for you, Tal, Jesus had said. I had no idea it would be this good.

I was on my way to meet Gia at the project site. She was helping me, and along the way I was training her to be an architect herself. At times I felt like an imposter—who was I to be teaching anyone? But I was surprised to find how much I had to share and how rewarding it felt to watch her grow and learn.

It was a beautiful, sunny day. Walking on the Gathering's busy, main trail, I suddenly heard my name.

"Tal?"

I turned around. A huge smile broke over my face.

"*Kenric!*"

I ran the few steps between us and hugged him—something that neither one of us would've done at the Rockface. "What are you doing here?"

"Well, a few weeks after you disappeared in the Cave, I took a big spill on the Rockface." He touched his left elbow. "A pretty nasty fracture."

"Are you okay?"

He chuckled as he held out his arm, which had a strange curvature to it. "I'm fine. Just a scar and an arm that won't go all the way straight. Ingrid and company took good care of me."

I felt a twinge of warmth and sadness shoot through me. "Awww, Ingrid. I miss her."

He nodded. "Me too, Tal. I don't think she realizes how much more Jesus has for her. Then again . . . neither did I." He smiled. "This trusting Jesus thing, it's better than I could've imagined. Harder, too. Better than the Field. Harder than the Rockface."

"You can say that again—to both." I grinned. "So, you gave up climbing after your fracture?"

Kenric laughed as he shook his head. "Not even close. Wow, was I stubborn. I was committed to climbing again. Actually, I had resolved to be a *better* climber to make up for the embarrassment of my fall!" He paused. "Then the craziest thing happened, Tal. On my first day back, I passed the Cave on my way to the Rockface. And I felt . . . something. Like a comforting breeze, but not, you know? Drawing me toward it." He laughed almost to himself. "I probably wouldn't have noticed it before the pain of my fall. But that day, I decided to follow it. I'm not even sure if that makes sense."

I smiled. "I think I know *exactly* what you mean. I call it the Windsong."

"The Windsong. I like that! Anyway, it was great to see you, Tal. I'd love to catch up more."

"You too, Kenric. I'm working on the new School Hall. Come by and see me sometime."

We hugged again. As I watched him walk away, I thought of the hand-painted banner that hangs high above the main road into the Gathering. It reads:

You could say that again. *Kenric! Here, at the Gathering!* I laughed to myself and shook my head. You really never knew what was around the bend.

When I arrived at the project site, Gia wasn't there yet. I set about cleaning and organizing materials at the school's future entrance. A few bypassers stopped and asked me questions about what was being built.

On my way around the backside of the construction site, I heard a few men talking in a building next door. Their voices drifted through an open window.

"I don't know. The plans for this School Hall just seem too . . . fancy and elaborate to me."

I froze. Wait.

I heard another voice. "My guess is they came from the upper class. Sometimes people like that have a hard time relating to common folk like us."

My heart started to beat painfully. They were talking about *me*.

Another man's voice rang out. "Well, it's *definitely* a Third Key design!" The group laughed.

It was like a stone dropped in my stomach. I knew that voice. *Aran.*

He was my friend. He was one of my mentors. He knew my story. He knew about the Wound. He had helped me care for it, and I had helped him. He was one of the few people who knew that I gave up three Keys at the Leap. And now he was making a joke of my design—of me. If *anybody* knew what the School Hall meant to me, it was Aran.

I turned away, my legs feeling far from my body. Shock was still in control but I could feel the wave of anger building behind it.

Gia jogged toward me frantically. "Tal, I'm so sorry I'm late! Tal? Tal!"

I walked past her. "It's fine, Gia. Don't worry about it. I gotta go." I just wanted to be alone.

"I got caught up in a conversation, and before I knew it . . . well, sorry. Are you, um, are you good to meet right now?"

But I was already walking away.

I kept my distance from Aran after that. Our conversations were brief. He clearly couldn't be trusted. He didn't even notice my withdrawal. Go figure. As construction on the School Hall progressed, so did my resentment toward him.

I felt less and less excited about the project. Every change I made or idea I proposed was drenched in insecurity. Was it too fancy? Did it seem too much like a "Third Key" design? At one point I considered making things as "common" as possible just to be passive-aggressive. But then my anger would come in. *Who cares what they think? If they were supposed to be in charge of this project, they would be!*

One morning I walked into the building, but only Aran was there. I turned to walk back out before he could notice me.

"Hey Tal!"

I closed my eyes briefly, took a deep breath and turned back toward him.

"Hi. How's it going in here?"

He walked toward me with a smile. "It's going great! It looks incredible. You're doing an amazing job."

Pretending to study a newly constructed part of the building, I ignored his comment. I knew it was fake.

He continued. "A few people have some modifications they want to propose for the entrance. You want to walk outside, and I'll show you what they suggested?"

Before I could stop myself, I snapped. "You know, Aran. No, I really *don't* want to hear anything from you. I'm sure you've had plenty of conversations with people about what I'm doing wrong behind my back, so how about this?" I threw my notebook on the table. "You be in charge. You call the shots! You obviously know the right, non-Third-Key way to do this. I'm done."

I slammed the newly-hung door on my way out.

A terrible storm of emotions was churning in my chest as I strode through the streets, not noticing where I was headed. Soon I found myself at the wide, expansive river that wove around the edges of the Gathering. I sat down angrily on the bank, brooding as I watched the fast-flowing current sweep by and thought of better insults I could've added.

I didn't even try to fight the velvet voice. It felt good to lean into it. *See, this is why you don't trust people. You thought this place was different. You thought Aran had grown and wouldn't hurt you again. These people say they follow Jesus? Doubtful. At least in Ican you knew to not trust anyone. Here they trick you into it!*

"Hello, Tal."

I closed my eyes. There were moments where the voice of Jesus was the last one I wanted to hear. This was one of them.

"Can we *please* not do this right now?" I said, keeping my eyes straight ahead as my anger bounced back and forth between anxiety and rage.

I heard the rustle of him sitting down next to me. The Windsong whispered around me, and I glared, hoping that would make it go away.

I knew I shouldn't be listening to the Shamesong, that velvet voice that had been stoking my resentment for weeks. But it felt better to cling to it. It felt more powerful than whatever was beneath it.

Jesus sat in silence, perfectly at ease with my fury.

I, on the other hand, was anything but comfortable. "Go ahead," I snapped, finally looking at him. "Tell me what I'm doing wrong and how I'm supposed to fix it."

"Why don't you start by telling me what happened." He leaned forward, his eyes intent. "Everything. How you've been feeling—even the stuff that feels petty or dramatic. I want to hear it all."

I huffed. "You already know it all, anyway."

He shook his head with a smile. "That's not the same as you telling me. Inviting me in."

I sighed. "A couple weeks ago, I was coming to inspect the progress for the School Hall. You know, the one Aran basically forced me to take on?"

On and on I went. At one point I was shouting, and I chucked a rock into the river. The ducks quacked and ruffled their feathers like they were offended, but Jesus just stayed locked in, nodding and frowning right alongside me.

Eventually, I ran out of steam. It did feel good to get it off my chest, to tell him everything that had been running around inside my head. "So that's it. I guess this is where you tell me I'm wrong or need to suck it up." I chucked another rock.

"Oh Tal." He shook his head with his voice full of compassion. "I never, ever tell you that you need to just suck it up or get over it. I'm so sorry that you've been hurt, and that it's made you question your friendship with Aran, your skill as an architect, and even this community in general. I feel that with you."

I closed my eyes and scratched my forehead irritably, fighting off the invitation in his tone. "Just explain why it's like this. Do people trust each other more only to get hurt more?"

He paused. "Yes."

I seethed. "So then what's the point? I took the Leap with only you. I walked into the Cave with only you. I can surely wear this Crest all by myself!"

He was silent for a moment, and then looked at me. "Yes, you can. But is that what you want?"

I laughed humorlessly. "Yes! Absolutely that's what I want!"

He stood up, beginning to pace along the bank. "I hate this, Tal! Almost as quickly as relationships were created here on earth, sin broke them.[1] And don't even get me started on the Shamesong." He shook his head in anger. "It's been hiding and dividing people from the beginning!"

I just flopped flat on my back, staring up at the clear sky. "Just tell me what I'm supposed to do already."

He chuckled at my vexation, and then sighed. "Tal, you have already taken the first big step. You're talking to me about it.[2] You're letting me in on your pain, frustration, and anger. Do you trust that I'm really hearing you? That I really understand and care deeply about how this affects you?"[3]

I stared at him a long moment before I answered. "You heard how he used my past against me, right? And used it to make fun of me to other people?"

Jesus nodded solemnly. "I know how much that hurt, Tal."

I let out a long breath. "Then yes. I trust that you hear me and that you care."

1. *Genesis 3:8-12*
2. *1 Peter 5:7*
3. *Psalm 34:18*

"Do you trust that I love you more than even *you* love you?"

That one pulled me up short. "What . . . what does that even mean?"

He smiled. "Do you trust that I want what is truly best for you and can see what is best for you even more than you can? That even when you abandon what's best for you, I never will?"

After some thought, I nodded. "Yeah. I do trust that."

"Do you trust that I love Aran in just the same way?"

I shrugged my shoulders. "Yeah."

"Okay. Then just right here, between you and me, would you hand over to me what Aran did, and let me hold it instead of you? Can you trust *me* with your hurt and anger and trust that I won't forget about it or discount it?"[4]

I sat up, gazing at the river in silence. Frustration grew as I thought about his words, and I finally grunted, "No, I actually *can't* do that. People who follow you are supposed to be different. But they're not. In fact, they're worse! At least in Ican people don't pretend to be all kind and loving. At least they're real."

The fire of my anger energized me, bringing me to my feet. "I'm sorry, but I don't want to forgive him, and I really don't want to talk about it anymore."

For the next few days, I did everything I could to ignore Jesus, the Windsong, and everyone else. I stayed in the Gathering out of pure stubbornness—I didn't want to give Aran the satisfaction of taking over *my* project—but I wasn't present. I was hurt by what Aran said, sure. But finding out that even here

4. Psalm 56:8

in the Gathering people talked behind each other's backs, betrayed each other, hurt each other? That devastated me.

This was supposed to be different, I thought to myself. *But it's a fantasy.* I saw every interaction in the Gathering through the filter of my disappointment. The Shamesong provided a supplemental message for each observation, piling them up like scar tissue around my heart. *Even if* God *is loving, this world sure isn't.* I felt a mixture of anger, sadness, and hopelessness, letting it all blend together into low-grade numbness. I was surprised at how quickly I could emotionally detach from . . . well, everything.

One day as I approached the School Hall, Gia was seated in the dirt, playing with a couple of children. I could see her, but she couldn't see me. A girl jumped into her lap, nearly knocking her over. Gia squeezed her with a playful growl and pointed toward the construction. "This is where you're going to school one day! My friend Tal is designing the *perfect* place for you!"

I felt something sharp pierce through my armor of numbness. I missed the joy of designing something for these kids. I missed Gia. I missed being close to people.

I stood there, paralyzed by my longing for the very thing that had hurt me. My feet started moving slowly toward the riverbank.

Jesus was there. As soon as I saw him, I threw my hands up in exasperation. "So why even bother with other people? Why can't you and I do this life thing alone?"

He smiled as I approached. "A lot of people try, Tal. But from the very beginning, it wasn't good for humans to be alone.[5] We made you for community. You need it."

I snorted. "I need it for *what?*"

"Well, let's see. To help you live in your true identity. To meet others' needs and have your needs met. To call each other in from the Wound of shame and toward the light. To love God by loving each other. To remind each other that you're beloved saints. To intercede for each other. Plus, there are many times that I choose to speak through and act through other people— it's kind of my thing."

He stopped and looked at me. Amusement played across his features. "Do you want me to continue? I can make this list as long as you want!"

My mind was racing. "So, what? I just let anybody do whatever they want? And no matter what, I just forgive them?"

He shook his head. "Being in community doesn't equal tolerating toxic relationships or abuse.[6] That's not love. Knowing what to say yes and no to doesn't mean you are unloving. And sometimes, those with Crests can hurt each other in terrible

5. *Genesis 2:18*
6. *Proverbs 22:24-25*

ways and then use *me* to justify their cruelty!" He took a deep breath, and I could feel his heartbreak and anger roll out like a storm cloud.

He closed his eyes briefly. "Things can get incredibly hurtful, messy, and destructive, Tal. I am working through people just like you to make it not so. But it doesn't change the fact that community is in your design. I made you for it. When you love others, you love me.[7] And when you refuse to give up on people, you show them how I love them, too."

I sighed. "You still want me to forgive him, don't you?"

Jesus nodded. "I want that burden off your shoulders. And I know what you're made for. Real connection is in your DNA."

"Okay. I . . . " I took another deep breath. "I trust that you know what's best. I trust that you really love me and are for me. So right here between you and I . . . I forgive Aran. I trust you to handle it." I felt a physical relief, the Windsong brushing by my ears.

Jesus' face broke into a joyful smile. "Thank you, Tal. Thank you for trusting me. I know it's not easy."

I laughed and wondered if everything came back to trust. "So what now?"

"Well, now, between you and me, you've forgiven Aran. And later you might realize some other effects of this hurt. You can come tell me about them, too. A lot of the time it's the *consequences* of what happened that are even more painful than the event itself. But now, you get the joy of offering forgiveness between you and Aran once he's ready. You see, people often feel like the safest relationships are those in which there is never any conflict. So if they have conflict with someone, their solution is to just go find new friends—or a new spouse. But actually,

7. I John 4:12; Matthew 25:40

your safest relationships come from being able to *repair* conflict.[8] This shows you that that relationship can withstand storms, not just sunny days. If you're willing to work through this with Aran, it can actually make your friendship stronger."

I turned to look back at the river. "Ugh. Sounds hard."

"Yeah. The best things often are."

"And I'm going to have to ask forgiveness for my outburst too, aren't I? And Gia."

"Right again. Unfortunately, the response to being hurt is often to hurt back."

We stood there in silence for a while, watching the river tumble by.

"I'm nervous," I finally told him quietly.

He smiled at me again and reached over and tapped my Crest. "It's okay to be nervous. But you don't have to be afraid, Tal. I will be with you, no matter how it goes."

---

8. Ephesians 4:32

Guide Notes

What if God designed you specifically for friendship?

The way of following Jesus is summed up as this: love God and love others. In fact, Jesus says that this is how people will know that we follow him.[9] Why are the "others" so important? As Jesus showed Tal, there are many reasons, but here's one of the biggest ones:

God designed you to grow in the context of friendships with God and others.

Friendships are more than just someone to enjoy (though they certainly are that, too). They are the place we live out, live in, and experience trusting Jesus. In friendship we practice love—both receiving it and giving it. We replace lies with truths about God and ourselves. We experience what it's like to be both known and loved.

In short, it's in relationships that we truly experience the beauty and power of what Jesus has done.

9. John 13:34-35

Don't miss how significant this is. Friendship is not a side addition to our walk with God. Friendship is rooted *in* God. After all, God is three Friends in one (the Trinity):

» God the Father
» God the Son
» God the Holy Spirit

The three Persons of the Trinity have been the closest of friends for, well, forever. They're the very best kinds of friends to us, too. Jesus calls us his friends, prays that we will experience the same unity that he has with the Father, and sends the Holy Spirit to dwell within us as a constant friend.[10] These amazing friends invite us into *their* friendship and to experience this same relationship with other humans.

Possibly the most cherished experience you will encounter on the Path is authentic, lasting friendships. Tal is beginning to experience this, and beginning to see that sometimes relationships that matter are messy.

The truth about friendship is that the closer we get to another, the more risk there is of being let down, betrayed, misunderstood, and even abandoned. Friendship is absolutely vital to our walk with Jesus. Friendship also carries an inherent risk of getting hurt. So what are we to do? Here are seven truths to lean into as you navigate this stunning, terrifying, glorious road of deep friendship.

---

10. *John 15:15; John 17:20-23; John 14:16-17*

1. Jesus was, and is, the best of friends.

A wisely chosen friend is "a friend who loves at all times."[11] This means in the good times, the bad times, and the routine times. Jesus experienced all of these times during his earthly life, including shiploads of betrayal and abandonment from his friends. Jesus knew all along he was laying himself open to hurt. And yet still . . .

> "Having loved his own who were in the world, he loved them to the end."[12]

Jesus is here for your best, worst, most joyful, most surprising, and least desired days. There is no place or time where he cannot and will not be present with you as the most faithful and very best friend. What kind of deity says to the subjects he created, "I no longer call you servants. Instead, I have called you friends"?[13] Only Jesus.

2. We are forever hardwired for deep friendships.

It was never good for humans to be without friendships. Even in paradise, "The LORD God said, 'It is not good for the man to be alone.'"[14] And don't miss this—man had *God* with him. It was man and God, palling around all day. And still, it was not good for man to be alone.

11. *Proverbs 17:17*
12. *John 13:1 (NIV)*
13. *John 15:15 (NIV)*
14. *Genesis 2:18 (NIV)*

Consider that even when Jesus—God in the flesh!—came to live with humans, he didn't travel alone. He became friends with the very people he created.

We can try to numb, minimize, or cover over this deep longing. Many of us have been deeply wounded in this area or struggle mightily to connect with others. Just like Tal with Rapha, allow God to tend to these wounds and fears, reminding you of who you are in him. Begin to pray for these God-given friends, and ask the Spirit to help you see opportunities for friendships. This need is in your very DNA!

3. We can only be loved to the degree we are known.

We can only experience love if we trust. When we show others a masked or "cleaned up" version of us, they are not really loving *us*. They are loving our mask. When we hide away parts of ourselves, it gives the Shamesong the fuel it needs to tell us, "They wouldn't love you if they *really* knew you." This shame and self-protection keep us from experiencing the full love of others.

As we learn to trust others, we allow them to know more and more of us. And as they know us more, they get to love us more—and we get to actually receive their love! Beware of the "last ten percent" that we often keep hidden away. This is often shame's favorite place to camp out. Find a few safe others that you can invite to know you *fully*. These are the kind of friendships you've longed for!

4. We mature in the context of friendships.

We cannot get healthy by ourselves. We were made to heal and mature through the love of others. God has designed us with a unique blind spot: ourselves. No matter how wise or mature we are, we need others to help us see ourselves clearly.

Without real, authentic relationships in our lives, we won't experience all that Jesus has for us or our full potential. We need the voices, perspectives, encouragements, challenges, and strengths of many others on our journey. Our destiny is revealed, refined, and matured in the context of these relationships.

5. Friendship is risky.

Anytime there's a gathering of people, there's a risk of being let down, left out, and misunderstood. People are human beings, and unfortunately this means that sometimes they'll mess things up. Wounded, imperfect people make for wounding, imperfect relationships . . . outside the church and inside the church.

People inside and outside the church forget birthdays, talk behind people's backs, and leave people out. They gossip and self-protect and have anger issues. They get defensive, avoidant, and dismissive. Sometimes, it actually hurts *more* when people in the church wound us—the church *should* be the most loving place in the world!

And yet the church is the Body of Christ. That means the church is you and me and anyone that has chosen to follow Jesus. And each one of us is still healing, learning, growing, and facing all of our own hangups and wounds. That means that even with the best of intentions, community *will* be messy.

6. Friendships take sacrifice.

Some years ago, the distinguished Tim Keller said this to his New York City audience:

> "If you love a nice person, a person whose life is all pulled together, everything's fine, and they don't need any changes. If you love someone like that it costs nothing. It's wonderful. It's fun. And, there are four or five of these people in New York City. You oughta find them and become their friends. But, if you ever try to love somebody who's got needs, who's got brokenness, who's got trouble or who is in trouble, who's persecuted, or emotionally wounded, it's going to cost you. You can't love them and bring them up without you going down. All real life-changing friendships require sacrifice."[15]

Jesus showed us this kind of friendship that requires sacrifice and extravagant love. He paid the ultimate price, loving us at our darkest,[16] to ensure (among other things) that we might begin to understand the magnificent meaning of friendship. He himself said, "Greater love has no one than this: to lay down one's life for one's friends."[17] Jesus' good friend John explains our response to this wild, extravagant love: "We love because

15. *Timothy Keller sermon, Redeemer Church, November 23, 2015.*
16. *Romans 5:8*
17. *John 15:13 (NIV)*

he first loved us."[18] If we are going to love our friends like Jesus does, it will require sacrifice.

7. Good friends heal hurts quickly.

One way that Jesus loved his sometimes selfish and dense friends during his time on earth was by rapidly and skillfully repairing ruptures. Perhaps the most famous rupture occurred when one of his closest friends, Peter, denied that he even knew Jesus at the very time when Jesus needed him most. Can you imagine this? The moment you most need your best friend to defend you or comfort you, they pretend they don't even know you.

What a gut drop.

When Jesus next sees Peter, he makes him breakfast and then opens a challenging, honest conversation, reassuring Peter of his friendship and love while inviting Peter to do the same. They repaired their friendship over good food and brave conversation. We can too. (Note: food isn't required, but it usually helps!)

Now, there are times when a rupture cannot or should not be repaired—times when abuse in a relationship or friendship is so severe and damaging or inherently dangerous that a necessary ending is best. But these are not the norm. Remember, Jesus has already made you new, beloved, holy, and accepted. We get to step into friendship from this place of security and love. When others let you down—and they will—Jesus reminds you that this does not change who you are.

This is what you were made for, dear friend.

18. I John 4:19 (NIV)

∽

Gia and the children were still playing outside the School Hall when I returned. I took a deep breath and walked straight up to her. "Gia, do you remember a few weeks ago when you showed up late to meet me here?"

She looked a little embarrassed and caught off guard by my forthrightness. I realized I probably should have started a little softer. "Yeah, uh, sorry again about that."

I waved her away. "I appreciate that, but I wasn't upset with you. I'm actually the one who needs to apologize. I was frustrated about something else, and I walked away while you were standing there. That couldn't have felt good."

I could see her shoulders relax. "Thanks Tal, I really appreciate that. I was worried you were angry with me, and I didn't know what to do about it. It kinda felt like that 'walking on eggshells' thing I told you about with my mom."

"Dang. I didn't even think about that," I shook my head. "I knew that about your story too. You *don't* deserve to be treated like that. I'm really sorry for being rude and for the worry you felt afterward. Will you please forgive me?"

She smiled. "Of course, Tal. As long as you'll forgive me for being late!"

"Absolutely," I laughed, relieved. There. The easier conversation was done. Now it was time for the harder one. "Have you seen Aran?"

"Yeah, he just went inside."

Aran had his back to me when I walked in, and I had to fight the instinct to run back out of the room. I took a deep breath, letting my fingers rest on my Crest. *You don't need to be afraid, Tal.*

"Hey Aran, can I talk to you?"

He looked around, clearly surprised to see me. "Oh, hey Tal. Um, sure," he replied nervously. I motioned for him to follow me and we walked back in the direction of the riverbank. I didn't see Jesus, but I knew he was with us.

I reminded myself that I had handed this over to Jesus, although my heart kept pounding uncomfortably. Finally, we stopped, and I turned to Aran. "Hey . . . I'm sorry about what happened earlier. That was really uncalled for."

"Thanks," he said, a little awkwardly. "Tal, is everything okay? I feel like you've been off lately."

I squinted out at the bright river. "Well actually, I've been kind of, I don't know, mad, I guess. I mean, I was upset because . . ." I was butchering this! "Do you remember a few weeks ago? Well . . ."

"Just say it, Tal."

I took a deep breath. "You were talking to a couple of guys in the building next to the School Hall. It was all about how my designs are too fancy and I don't understand how to build things for common people. You said that it was definitely a 'Third Key type of design.' I told you about being a Third Key in confidence—you know it's not something I'm comfortable with a lot of people knowing. Plus, you were using it to make me the butt of a joke. I felt . . . " I searched my mind for a moment, "betrayed, I guess. Like that gut-drop moment when you realize your friends are making fun of you behind your back."

I felt embarrassed and vulnerable just saying it out loud.

It was like handing a knife back to someone who just stabbed me, and then telling them how much it hurt last time.

"Oh, wow," Aran replied, alarmed and concerned. "I mean, I don't even remember saying that. Are you sure you heard me right?"

I paused. I could feel his defenses rising, and my anxiety with it. "Yeah, Aran . . . I heard you right."

He ran his hands through his hair, his mind obviously racing. Then his head turned sharply toward me, frowning. "Wait— you were eavesdropping on me?"

I was shocked for a moment. "Not on purpose! Trust me, I wish I hadn't heard what you were saying."

He was obviously agitated, quasi-pacing back and forth. "I mean that was clearly a private conversation that you were listening to, and now you're turning it into this big deal."

I felt anxiety grip my body. "Aran, if you think that taking a part of my story that I didn't want you to share with others— and not only telling it, but turning it into a joke—*isn't* a big deal, then I really don't know you the way I thought I did."

Aran stopped and shook his head. "Wow, seriously? Look, you've obviously blown this up in your head. And now apparently I can't do anything right. How about I just give you some space so you can calm down?"

And with that, he turned and walked off.

I sat down on the ground and stared numbly at the river. *Wow, that really went awful.* I let my hand rest on my Crest, struggling to trust Jesus. *I said what I needed to say. I've done what I can.*

I probably sat at the river's edge for an hour. Part of me felt stupid for even trying—I ended up getting more hurt. Part of me was trying to trust Jesus with the outcome. Part of me wanted to just move on and accept that our friendship was over.

I finally stood up. I was tired of replaying it over and over.

"Tal," I heard Aran's voice as I finished dusting myself off. His hair was standing up on end as he jogged up, out of breath. "I'm so glad you're still here."

Oh gosh. I didn't want to do this again. Once was enough. "It's fine, Aran. It's whatever. We don't need to talk about it."

"No, I'm sorry." He looked at me imploringly. "I . . . I can get a little defensive." I frowned at him. "Okay, really defensive. I've been working on it, but it usually comes out of my mouth before I even realize it's happening. I knew I was going to mess this up. And I did. What I said to you earlier was stupid—I was just freaked out and trying to cover up. Can we sit?"

I sighed, teetering. "Sure," I finally shrugged.

We sat down, and Aran seemed to compose himself for a moment. "I have to be honest, Tal, I really *don't* remember that conversation. Like, at all. I trust that if that's what you heard, then that's what I said, and I can imagine how much that would hurt. I feel confident that I wasn't meaning to make fun of you, but I clearly shared private information when I shouldn't have. And that's just . . . " He shook his head, more to himself than to me. "I feel a lot of shame about that. That was messed up. I'm so sorry. Here's what I *do* know. I'm so proud of you and your talent, and I'm so proud to be your friend. I'm so sorry that whatever I said hurt you, and I own that."

I quickly scrubbed my face to avoid the emotion that came up. I said reflexively. "It's fine. Don't worry about it."

"No, Tal. It's not. It's not fine," he held my gaze and said it confidently. "You felt betrayed because of something I said. I care so much about you and our friendship. Please forgive me."

I looked at his face and thought of the pain I had felt the last few weeks. And I thought of all the laughter and deep talks and side-by-side adventures. I believed him. I believed he was sorry and that he took my pain seriously. I believed we could build back our trust.

The Windsong swept along the river as I nodded and smiled. "I forgive you, Aran."

Selah

You may let others see your house. Look in your windows. Perhaps even view—from afar—that vase that you mended or the laundry you have yet to fold and put in its place. They can see, but not touch. Stop by, but not enter. Understand, but certainly not handle.

Transparency at its finest.

But perhaps you trusted someone enough to let them enter. To walk on your floors with shoes that might carry their own dust.

To get close enough to that vase to see there are still jagged cracks in it.

To even reach out and touch it as you hold your breath, wondering if they will smash it to pieces or tenderly help you mend it.

Vulnerability at its most glorious and terrifying.

Who is allowed in the house of your heart? Who might you—despite the nervous beat of your heart—invite inside?

THE GIFTS

What is essential is life with Jesus, interactive relationship with the great God of the universe, inner transformation into Christlikeness.

—RICHARD FOSTER

We are not the first journeyers on this Path. We will not be the last. Ahead and behind we see the footprints of those who have traveled this glorious Way for millenia. Long ago, the One who forged this way through the wilderness, the first to travel its twists and turns, began to teach us how to travel well. Practices to help train our minds, bodies, and spirits to trust, to listen, to follow. He showed us rhythms of doing and not doing, of stillness and action, of releasing and grasping.

And today he invites us to join him still, calling us forward: "Follow me."[1]

1. *Matthew 4:19; Mark 2:14; Luke 9:59*

∽

It seemed like any normal Tuesday afternoon. Kenric had just joined our team, and we were mixing mortar for a new addition to the inn.

"Tal!" Aran waved as he walked up. "There's a man north of town who wants to see you about his house. His name is . . . " He checked the sheet he was holding. "Nahal. Says here he's about a half mile outside of town. The house with two chimneys."

I straightened, dusting my hands off. "What's he need?"

Aran consulted the sheet again, "Some kind of remodel consultation."

"Interesting." I thought for a moment. "What do you say, Kenric? Want to go?"

He was carefully setting his tools aside, lining them up meticulously. "Honestly I'd love to, but I'm making a guest appearance at the School Hall today. Going to share my story of the Rockface."

"Hey, that's a big deal!" I clapped him on the shoulder even as he grimaced. I knew he was nervous. "You've been putting that off for a while. I'm proud of you."

He heaved a deep breath and nodded. "I'll let you know how it goes."

I grabbed my sketchbook and headed up the road.

The road wound between rolling hills covered in bright spring grass. Eventually I saw two chimneys rising up over the next crest, and soon enough the rest of the house appeared, nestled perfectly between two hills.

"This guy definitely *doesn't* need a Master Architect," I muttered to myself as I headed up the stone walkway. The house was quaint, charming, and designed with simplicity and strength. An elderly man with long white hair sat whittling on the porch.

"Hello, Tal!" he called. "Welcome to my place!"

"Nice to meet you, Nahal." I shook his hand then gestured around us. "Your place is incredible."

"Thank you. Been in the family a long time. Can I get you some coffee and a snack?"

"Sure! Thanks." It had taken a while to get used to how relational many people were in the Gathering. I was trying to learn how to slow down and sit with people instead of just immediately jumping to the work.

Nahal, on the other hand, seemed like a natural at this as we talked and ate on his front porch. He asked me questions about my work, and we chatted about the recent storms. There was something about Nahal's house—and Nahal himself—that made me feel comfortable and easy.

"So what do you do, Nahal?"

He shrugged, "A little of this, a little of that." He winked. "I've had many different calls in my life. In this season, I keep this house," he gestured behind him, "and offer it as a place for people to rest. Sometimes people just need to sit or whittle or talk things through with an old guy like me. I help them learn the rhythms of grace that Jesus taught."

I sat in silence for a moment, reflecting on how easy it already was to open up to him. "I bet I could learn a lot from you, Nahal."

"As I'm sure I could from you!" He smiled and stood up. "And I could sit and talk all day. It's actually my one and only superpower. But I know you're busy, friend. So let me show you why I called you out here."

Nahal led me to the backside of his property just before the land sloped upward into the foothills of the mountains. There stood the remnants of an overgrown, dilapidated, and abandoned shack.

"This was my great, great grandfather's house. His son—my great grandfather—started construction on the house I live in today, and my grandfather completed it. I don't think he or my father stepped foot in this structure very often, nor have I. I can't say that I'm 'tearing it down,' because my father would roll over in his grave. So here's what I *am* saying. I want to preserve what can be preserved and build a little guest house in its place for visitors who pass through."

I surveyed the falling-down structure and could already see the possibilities. It took me back to all those years ago, trying to imagine a gazebo in my small town square. "Well, there's a lot of people that need rest and some time with an old guy like you." I grinned at him. "So let's build you a little guest house, shall we?"

∾

Two weeks later I was gently prying up the few floor planks that weren't rotted in Nahal's shed. I had been trying to preserve what I could, honoring Nahal's family, but the "keep" pile was still pretty small.

With a grunt I pried a plank loose, and as I picked it up something below caught my eye. I knelt down, gently wiggling out a small wooden box that had been concealed under the boards. As I blew some of the dust off, I saw that it had been carefully carved, covered in garden imagery. *Whittling must have run in the family*, I thought to myself.

"I'll admit, I was curious," I announced as I climbed the steps to Nahal's front porch a few minutes later. "But I promise I didn't look inside."

His eyes lit up as I handed him the box. "Where did you find this?"

"Under some floorboards in the old house."

He gently ran his hand over the dusty carvings. "I never thought I'd see this again," he murmured. "Now how did it . . . " His fingers worked over the carvings until a gentle "pop" sounded.

"Hidden latch," he said, smiling. I could feel my anticipation rising. What was this?

Gingerly, he opened the box. Inside was a small, ancient-looking book. Although its red, velvet cover was simple, it was somehow captivating. Magical. Nahal ran his finger over the worn edges and folds.

Nahal's voice shook a little when he spoke. "*The Gifts*. I thought this book was gone forever." He shook his head. "So

many memories of my grandfather reading this to me when I was just a boy. We would sit in front of the fire, and he would read from this very book. I can't imagine why he put it under the floor of the old house."

I remained silent, studying Nahal. He looked back at me. "Do you think it's a coincidence that you found this book, Tal?"

Again I kept silent as I stared at the worn pages. A humming was starting in my bones.

"But what *is* it, Tal?" Gia asked, trotting to keep up.

I laughed. "I genuinely don't know! He just told me to get my friends and he'd share it with us." I looked around at her, Kenric, and Aran, "Sorry, but that means you three are roped into this, too."

Kenric laughed. "He didn't say anything else?"

I smiled to myself as my eyes trained on the two chimneys in the distance. "He just said to be adventurously expectant," I looked over at Kenric and we grinned. "That was enough for me."

Nahal ushered us into the living room as soon as we arrived. The smell of coffee and lemon cake greeted us. He began asking us questions as he poured the coffee, but Kenric couldn't contain himself.

"But tell us about this mysterious book Tal found," he cut in before Nahal could ask him anything else.

Nahal laughed. "Oh, that old thing?" His eyes twinkled as he teased us. "Alright, alright. I *am* excited to share this with you."

He brought the worn book over to the wooden table, and we all leaned in as he ran his fingers over the soft cover.

"This book lays out timeless practices of spiritual growth," he said wistfully. "Jesus followers have been using these Gifts for thousands of years to help remind them of what is true: what is true about God, and what is now true about them." His hand rested on his Crest. "This book is where I began to learn the rhythms of grace that Jesus showed us."

Aran spoke up, "Why are they called Gifts, Nahal?"

"Good question. Because they're not accomplished or earned—they're received and enjoyed. My grandfather called them 'the Gifts of the Windsong.'"

Gia smiled, "That's beautiful, Nahal." She paused. "But . . . I still feel confused. These Gifts, what do we . . . do with them?"

"You open them and use them just like any other gift. You practice them together, share them, and talk about them."

The word *practice* piqued our interest. Kenric sensed the anticipation that buzzed around the table. "With all due respect, Nahal, this sounds a lot like scaling the mountain. And as a recovering Scaler, I could see myself going in a not-great direction with this."

Nahal laughed. "I'm a recovering Scaler too, Kenric! Listen, we're daily, constantly presented with the choice of trying to do more ourselves and scale the Rockface, sit passively in the Field, or trust Jesus as we venture into the Cave. These gifts offer rhythm to the music of trusting Jesus."

"Ohhh so these are the dance moves that go with the Windsong," Gia replied and we burst out laughing.

After a few moments I said, "Okay, Nahal. I think you've drawn it out long enough. Let's hear about these Gifts."

Nahal nodded and stood up, gently opening to the first page. He cleared his throat.

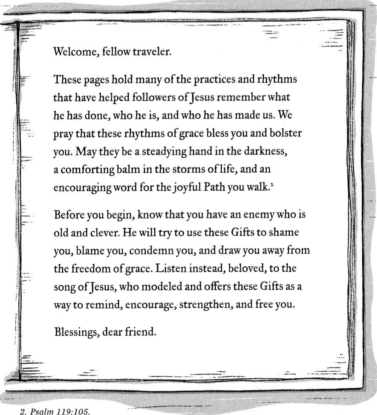

Welcome, fellow traveler.

These pages hold many of the practices and rhythms that have helped followers of Jesus remember what he has done, who he is, and who he has made us. We pray that these rhythms of grace bless you and bolster you. May they be a steadying hand in the darkness, a comforting balm in the storms of life, and an encouraging word for the joyful Path you walk.[2]

Before you begin, know that you have an enemy who is old and clever. He will try to use these Gifts to shame you, blame you, condemn you, and draw you away from the freedom of grace. Listen instead, beloved, to the song of Jesus, who modeled and offers these Gifts as a way to remind, encourage, strengthen, and free you.

Blessings, dear friend.

2. Psalm 119:105.

Nahal gently turned the page. The crinkle of the paper was the only sound in the room. "The first Gift," he read out, "is prayer."

I stared at the words on the page, but my mind was anywhere but on them.

I shook my head for the eighth time. The river rushed beside me, merrily dancing along the rocks and pebbles. Overhead was a crystal clear sky and the sun just warm enough to balance the light breeze. I had chosen this spot specifically to practice the Gift of studying scripture because I thought it would be peaceful and contemplative.

So why was my mind jumping all over the place? I couldn't stop thinking about all my to-dos and my upcoming projects.

I rubbed my eyes in frustration and wondered if I was the only one struggling. Tomorrow was Monday, the day Aran, Kenric, Gia and I would meet at Nahal's home to learn about one of the Gifts and then practice it together. This week we were practicing the Gift of studying God's written scriptures.

We had started with **prayer**. *The Gifts* described prayer as simply talking with God and listening to him. We practiced praying together and alone, out loud and in our minds. Our prayers were short, long, full of emotion, or full of confusion. We all worried whether we were doing it "right"—and reminded each other that that wasn't the point.

"Ahem." Gia had cleared her throat, standing up from the table and reading the page out loud. "'Fellow travelers, we are designed for a relationship with God, and prayer is part of that relationship. It changes from day to day, from season to season.

It is more dynamic, mysterious, and wonderful than any formula or method.'"

She looked around our circle. "I'm pretty sure that's just saying there's no wrong way to do it. Just . . . keep talking." We laughed. "And listening."

Next, we had learned about and practiced **worship**. We worshiped with a song, with our efforts, with reciting scripture, and with our affection. Kenric and I would remind each other to look at our work as an act of worship.[3] Anything that turned our hearts toward God and celebrated his character was considered worship.

The following week we practiced **generosity**. We gave away time, money, or energy on behalf of others.[4] Under Nahal's direction, we began renovating the house of an elderly woman to make it suitable for her growing physical challenges. Generosity reminded us that as we receive so generously from God and each other, we get to overflow with love and meet the needs of others. We found so much affirmation in generosity that we often had to remind each other that it *wasn't* our primary identity. We'd encourage each other to not get so lost in giving love that we failed to receive it and to not get so overwhelmed by meeting others' needs that we forgot to stop and recharge.[5]

After that we began practicing **solitude**. It was a way of creating space to experience God's presence in a habitual and intentional way.[6] We struggled at first—our minds felt like they couldn't slow down—but over time we grew to cherish the time to pause and listen to God. **Sabbath** rest was the Gift that reminded us of our limitations and dependence on God—that

3. *Colossians 3:17*
4. *Hebrews 13:16*
5. *Mark 6:31-32*
6. *Luke 5:16*

being with him was far more important than doing *for* him.[7]
Fasting increased our awareness of our primary desire for God,
which was even greater than our desire for food.[8]

And then this week we had begun learning about studying
God's written word, and I was about ready to chuck the book
of scriptures into the river. It just wasn't connecting with me.

I doubled down on my concentration, trying to force my
heart to be affected by the words on the page. *What's wrong
with me?*

And then I heard it.

It took me a second to recognize the subtle key, but it
slowly echoed around me. The velvet voice. It was hard to tell
where my thoughts ended and its sultry tone began. *This is
pathetic, Tal. After all God has shown you, you can't even read
his Word for five minutes?* And then it was so strong that I felt

7. *Hebrews 4:9-10*
8. *Matthew 4:2-4*

like it was talking to me out loud. *Try harder, Tal! Get serious. Everyone else is.*

I snapped the book closed as anxiety flooded me.

I needed my friends.

Nahal was seated on his porch, but the rest of us stood. Gia, who had been pacing back and forth, spoke first. "I don't get it, Nahal. I thought these were supposed to be gifts, but some days they feel like a boring curse." She looked around at us. "You guys know that I lived in the Field for a while—that's where I start to lean when I forget to trust Jesus. And sometimes these Gifts feel like the exact reason I wanted to stay in the Field! They can be so difficult."

"Yeah, it's the weirdest thing," Kenric agreed as he pushed off the railing. "You know I lean the other way, towards striving, so I can easily feel like I'm not measuring up. Like serving— some days I come alive working with the kids at the School Hall. Other days I'm hit from multiple angles. On one hand, I feel guilty for not doing more. On the other hand, I'm so annoyed at a few of the kids that I want to just quit!"

We all laughed. We knew exactly which kids he was referring to.

Aran took his turn. "I'll be honest, I've been struggling with some of these. I critique my prayers as I say them—some of them sound so stupid as I say them! I even critique *other people's* prayers. I'm absolutely terrible at resting and fasting. Actually, I feel like I'm pretty terrible at all of this." He sat down in a huff as the wooden chair creaked beneath him. I knew how he felt.

Nahal smiled. "Can I just pause here and say how proud I am of each of you for trusting us with how you're really feeling?" Nahal looked at Aran, who narrowly avoided rolling his eyes. Nahal smiled like he knew it. "Your worst aspects can be known by safe friends, Aran. You will be loved more, not less, by opening up. And how you feel is *exactly* how I felt when I started practicing the Gifts. Actually, it's still how I feel sometimes!" He shrugged. "But I know that's just my shame talking."

Nahal looked at me, the only one who hadn't spoken yet. I looked anxiously around the circle.

"I don't know," I said. "Some days have felt so good, like they really were gifts. Others . . . not so much. Yesterday I was trying to study by the river. But it was like the more I tried, the harder it got. I didn't hear the Windsong—I heard the *other* voice. The deceiver. Pretty loudly, actually. It freaked me out. It told me I was pathetic and not trying hard enough. It felt so true. Like I was failing God."

Nahal stood up and put his hands on both my shoulders. "Tal, thank you for telling us." He stared seriously into my eyes for a moment. "And that is absolute crap."

Shocked laughter skittered around the porch. I couldn't help but grin.

Nahal's face turned serious again. "Lies from hell, Tal. You are a loved child of God, and some days it just feels hard to study. That doesn't change who you are just like studying doesn't change who you are. These Gifts help us *experience* more of who we are, not change it."

Kenric argued, "But then why do they feel like such a struggle some days?"

Nahal replied, "That's what all journeys have, Kenric—*some* days. Some good, some bad. Some happy, some sad. Some easy, some difficult. The point is that we stay in it. It's not on you—we know that *God* will complete the good work he started in each of us.[9] We don't complete it by our good efforts. Our job is to trust him and follow him. These Gifts help us receive and remember that."

I couldn't help but ask, "But why would we make ourselves more susceptible to shame, Nahal? Now that I think about it, I heard it in almost every Gift at some point."

"We're susceptible to shame no matter what we do or don't do, Tal. We have the best hero out there, but we also have a fierce enemy who doesn't like going down without a fight.[10] The battle has already been won, but that doesn't mean he won't take something beautiful and try to use it to beat us up."

We were all quiet for a moment. Gia finally asked, "So what do we do?"

"You do exactly what you're already doing, Gia. Keep processing things together, and remember that the responsibility of maturing you belongs to Jesus, not you."

After a moment of quiet contemplation, I stepped forward. "Alright, I think it's my turn—finally." That earned a few laughs. I picked up the worn book and cleared my throat. "'Today, dear travelers, we will be experiencing the holy practice of communion together.'"

9. *Philippians 1:6*
10. *I Peter 5:8*

Guide Notes

What if the greatest spiritual practice is letting Jesus love you?

We are all being formed spiritually just like we are being formed physically.

What we eat, how we exercise, and our rhythm of sleep are all forming us physically either positively or negatively. Ice cream or vegetables. Watching another show or working out. These choices, unfortunately, lead to different results.

While we might have all the muscles, ligaments, and joints to be able to run a marathon, we still need to train in order to healthily run the race. Simply thinking about running a marathon won't get us very far. Training, on the other hand—that would help.

In a similar way, all people have an inner spirit that is being formed into something. We are affected by the rhythms and influences that we surround ourselves with. As sons and daughters of Jesus, we have all of his love, joy, peace, and patience fused within us already, but we need to train in order to *experience* these attributes as we run the race of life.[11]

Many of us want to experience spiritual growth. We want to experience a more real and connected relationship with Jesus. We just aren't sure *how*. This is where the Gifts come in. They've been called many things—rhythms of grace, spiritual disciplines, holy habits, discipleship practices ... but really they are beautiful relational gifts that help us mature.

Wait, is this just back to the Rockface of striving?

Just like Tal, Gia, Kenric, and Aran experienced, it's vital that we practice these rhythms with the right mindset. It's far too easy to slip into a damaging one here. As you begin to engage with the Gifts, are you getting pulled from effort into *earning*? Here are some questions to help you:

» Are these practices compulsions you feel you need to do to please God or others in your life?
» Are they making you feel superior to other Jesus followers? Is your experience of them (or lack thereof) making you feel worse than others?
» Do these rhythms help or interfere with you loving others?

11. *I Timothy 4:8; I Corinthians 9:24-27*

» Would you recommend these practices to a friend because you feel like "good Christians" should be doing these things?
» Are they aimed at improving yourself or enjoying God?

We do not use these Gifts to please a deity or make ourselves okay with God. Jesus already accomplished that for us. Nor do we use them to arrive at a higher level of spirituality. You cannot get more holy, more righteous, or more beloved than you already are.[12] But, you can experience maturing into the saint you already are!

Remember, the relational gifts only have value if they bring us to Jesus. Not to Jesus as a concept, but as a Person who loves us passionately. As we get to know this Person, we will experience more and more of what is already true: that he himself is the life within us.[13]

Relational Rhythms

Imagine a married couple. They've been married for ten years, and they are committed to live the rest of their lives together. These might be accurate facts about their relationship, but it doesn't tell us anything about the *quality* of it.

They might trudge through the next fifty years disappointed, disconnected, and disillusioned. They're still married, but they don't experience the joy, connection, and flourishing that God intended for marriage. If they *do* want to have a

---

12. *II Corinthians 5:21, Colossians 3:12*
13. *Romans 8:10*

healthy, fulfilling marriage, they will identify ways to prioritize each other and their relationship. This might look like:

» Eating dinner together at least four nights a week.
» Laughing and having fun together.
» Taking walks.
» Looking for activities to enjoy together.
» Reading and discussing the same book.
» Working on projects together.
» Setting aside specific times to talk honestly about their relationship.
» Getting away together to connect every few months.

These rhythms help couples experience deeper friendship, grow together, and stay more connected.

Are they rules a couple must follow? No, of course not.

If they miss a day, will they have to feel bad about it? No.

Or how about this: Does any one married couple do all of these things? Probably not. Each couple is different. Therefore, each marriage is different. Some practices and rhythms that are meaningful to one couple may not be meaningful to another. Every married couple picks and chooses what helps *them* experience connection.

These are relational rhythms. Couples do these things together for two reasons:

1. They enjoy being together so they naturally want to.
2. They know that prioritizing their relationship, day in and day out, will help them have the best possible marriage.

What gifts! Spiritual practices are no different. God also knows that having a relationship with someone we don't see or hear audibly isn't very easy or simple . . . especially in a busy, physical world. He knows that we need rhythms and practices to continue deepening our relationship with him.

Jesus knew this. While here on earth, he modeled these relational rhythms, enjoying his Father and prioritizing their relationship above all else. Over the past two thousand years, Christians have been following after Jesus and practicing his way of living through these same rhythms. Per usual, Jesus has the best invitation into these ways of living . . .

Are you tired? Worn out? Burned out on religion? Come to me. Get away with me and you'll recover your life. I'll show you how to take a real rest. Walk with me and work with me—watch how I do it. Learn the unforced rhythms of grace. I won't lay anything heavy or ill-fitting on you. Keep company with me and you'll learn to live freely and lightly.

—MATTHEW 11:28-30, (MSG)

So what are these Gifts, and which ones should I use?

These spiritual expressions have been practiced by Jesus followers for millennia across different cultures and contexts, languages and locations. And yet, they are also personal and unique to each of us.

Dallas Willard classified spiritual disciplines into two main types: Disciplines that help us exercise our "doing" muscles, and disciplines that help us exercise our "not doing" muscles. We might think of these as Gifts of Being and Gifts of Engaging.

Gifts of Being:

" . . . he said to them, 'Come with me by yourselves to a quiet place and get some rest.'"

—MARK 6:31 (NIV)

Gifts of Being are practices where you step away from certain activities in order to delight in God. We practice *not* doing. For many of us this is uncomfortable. We don't like silence, solitude, or rest (all spiritual disciplines). They make us uncomfortable and even anxious. This is precisely why they are so valuable to our souls! If you find yourself typically drawn to the Rockface of Striving, Gifts of Being might be especially difficult—and especially powerful—for you. Refraining from things like distraction (silence), food (fasting), sex (chastity), company (solitude), and consuming (frugality) can help reorient us to the way that God meets us in our needs. It helps remind us that God first desires our presence *with* him more than our activity *for* him.

Gifts of Engaging:

"For we are his workmanship, created in Christ Jesus for good works, which God prepared beforehand, that we should walk in them."

—EPHESIANS 2:10 (ESV)

Gifts of Engaging help us engage in activities that foster spiritual growth. For those of us who lean more towards the Field of Passivity, we might wrestle with using these "doing" muscles, making Gifts of Engagement deeply impactful for us. These gifts help us mature in our faith, deepen our understanding of God's truths, and build a supportive community of believers. God uses them to help us step into a deeper, more vibrant spiritual life. These look like prayer, worship, study, service, fellowship, celebration, and more. These help us engage in the good work God has prepared for us.

These Gifts of Being and Engaging add to the mystery and adventure of following Jesus as you learn and experience new ways to receive his love. Jesus knew the blessing of these Gifts because *he experienced them*. We see Jesus practicing the Gifts throughout his life on earth and teaching his disciples how to do so as well.[14] He knew that we would need rhythms to help us experience a direct, veil-is-torn relationship with God.[15]

Through practice, you will discover which Gifts help you experience God's love and presence in various seasons of your faith journey.

14. Mark 1:35; John 17:1-5; Luke 4:2-4; Matthew 6:1-21
15. Matthew 27:51

An Antidote for Lies

One of the amazing attributes of these spiritual rhythms is the way they help us see through and overcome deception in our lives. Spiritual growth happens as we replace lies with truth.[16] Here are a few examples of how practicing the Gifts can help us reorient to truth.

» **LIE: In God's economy, I get what I put in.**
» TRUTH: The Gifts help us remember that spiritual growth happens as I receive not achieve. We can only show up and engage; God is in charge of the rest.

» **LIE: I cannot slow down.**
» TRUTH: The Gifts help us to pause and set aside our control-focused goals and activities in favor of trusting Jesus' pace and provision.

» **LIE: If I can figure _____ out, I will finally overcome my anxiety.**
» TRUTH: These spiritual expressions invite us to receive God's love and care in the midst of confusion and fear. They are not tools to overcome our emotions but ways we experience love in the midst of them.

16. Romans 12:2; John 8:31-32; Ephesians 5:8-14

» **LIE: God wants me to be comfortable above all.**

» TRUTH: Many of these Gifts require discomfort or sacrifice. Spending time studying when you'd rather stay in bed is challenging, and fasting contains plenty of intentional discomfort. God desires our *good* above all, and sometimes that's uncomfortable.

» **LIE: My walk with God is a solo journey.**

» TRUTH: These practices are collective in their nature. Some of them are enjoyed best in community, and as we've seen with Tal, we often need trusted friends to help us practice them. When we engage in these ancient practices, we join in with believers throughout the ages, affirming God's love and presence with us all.

The Greatest Gift

Remember: Jesus is not inviting you to put in effort to gain favor with God or become a new person. You're *always* walking in God's favor because Jesus has already secured all of his Father's favor for you. You are a brand new creation: finished and completed, full-stop. Of all the Gifts, this is THE foundational, one-time-forever-settled Gift: your identity in Christ.

Perhaps the greatest joy that the Gifts offer is the space to let Jesus just love you.[17] Fight the temptation to overthink or over-spiritualize this. Find where your heart more naturally connects with the Father. That's what Jesus seems to have done.

Perhaps for you this is going for a hike or sitting with a good

17. *Psalm 46:10*

early morning coffee or late nights by the fire reading. Just like we prefer connecting with our friends in different ways, each of us will have our own ways that we prefer being with God.

He is the most personal God. He simply wants time with you. There is nothing like sitting and soaking in the love and care of Jesus for you. Devoting time to this will counter lies better than anything in the universe.

Selah

Now's a good time to pause. To be still. To listen to the rhythms around you—breathing and beating. Opening and closing. Thinking and feeling.

Do your muscles long to move, to do, to achieve?
Breathe. Slow.

Do they long to be left alone, at rest but unused?
Lift up your gaze.

And in the midst, there's an invitation—again.
To trust—again.

As Jesus invites you to travel deeper, what practice does your heart require?

THE STORY

*The place God calls you to is the place where your deep gladness
and the world's deep hunger meet.*

—FREDERICK BUECHNER

Every morning we stand on the wild edge of a story unfolding beneath our very feet.

The wonderful and sometimes bewildering King we follow is the Master Storyteller, weaving the individual threads of our lives into the very tapestry of the cosmos. From the beginning of time to the end, he has conducted this orchestra of life and breath and sorrow and death into his song of redemption and love.

Dear traveler, today you are playing a collection of notes that you may not understand in this moment—or perhaps in this lifetime. But know that one day, when you sit by his side and listen to the music of the Kingdom, you will rejoice in the integral part that you played.

∾

"Yes, I think this should work," I told Gia as I looked over her drawings. "We'll need Aran's leadership for the timeline and materials. But I think this is the best way to provide more housing."

I looked up at Gia and caught her grinning.

"What?" I asked.

"It's just cool to see how God's using you, Tal." She shrugged. "I don't know, not what I expected."

"You're telling me." I thought for a moment. "Remember when we very first came to the Gathering? And I apprenticed under that farmer?"

She laughed. "Oh yeah. Wow, I forgot about that. You were so sure that you should have nothing to do with architecture or building."

"Yep." I leaned back. "I thought that would be like going back to Ican. And working with the farmer was an awesome season of my life. There was something about getting to be so in touch with the land that was really . . . I don't know. Healing for me."

I remembered the day Aran came out to meet me at the farm. He had gently and firmly challenged me on why I wasn't using my talents. He had pointed out how much fear was in my answers.

"You know, Tal, there's this section of scripture that I have always loved, and I feel like it applies here," he had told me. "It says, 'This resurrection life you received from God is not a timid, grave-tending life. It's adventurously expectant, greeting God with a childlike "What's next, Papa?"'[1] I really think

1. Romans 8:15 (MSG).

using your talents as a Master Architect might be what's next. Promise me you'll pray about it, okay?"

Adventurously expectant. I shook my head with a smile. That sure came up a lot around here.

I had thought about Aran's points and felt the Spirit nudging me forward into something strange and wonderful. That's how I had ended up designing and building the new School Hall, and then renovating Nahal's house and finding *The Gifts*. Now my work had morphed into wider-reaching building plans, trying to help Aran and the town council figure out how to make sure everyone had reliable housing. New Crest-bearers were arriving every day, and they needed places to live.

Gia smiled and gathered up the papers, slipping naturally into the Gift of prayer. "God, thank you for how you have shaped each of our lives. It's so cool to see how you lead us and guide us in different seasons. Thanks especially for my friend, Tal!"

I leaned back in the chair after she left, thinking about how God had given me talents even before I chose to follow him. Now he had invited me to use them in his Kingdom.[2] It felt good. Right. The Windsong hummed in the background as I collected my things from the table. I felt my spirit longing for the rhythm of solitude, and I thought I'd take a quiet walk.

I wound my way through the streets, dodging sprinting children and waving to friends. *You know, when you're following a wild God, you never know what the next day is going to bring,* I thought to myself. Not that there hadn't been many ordinary-seeming days. It was more that I was beginning to see the incredible story that God had been writing even before I knew he existed. He had been weaving together my talents and

2. *Ephesians 2:10; I Corinthians 12:4-6*

struggles and joys and wounds to get me here for this work. I shook my head. Wild indeed!

"Alright, we're going to need to reinforce this whole section," I told Aran as we walked carefully through the old Medical Hall. It was literally falling apart and hadn't been safe enough to use for at least a year. "Are you sure we can't just tear it down and build a new one?"

Aran shook his head. "The town council says we don't have the budget for that right now. We can only do phase renovations." I grunted, and Aran smiled. "I know, not your favorite. But it's what we can do."

"I don't think it's so bad," Gia separated from the other workers we had brought, slowly walking around the room. "We can spruce this place up."

"Sounds like someone's ready for their first Lead project," I grinned. Gia's eyes went wide.

"Nope, definitely not ready for that!"

I chuckled, walking over to the old entrance. The bones were here. Just needed a ton of help. I ran my hand over the exposed wood, wondering how long it had been there. Who had put it up in the first place?

"Tal!"

I started to turn, but I was too late. I felt the beam's impact right before I was knocked out cold.

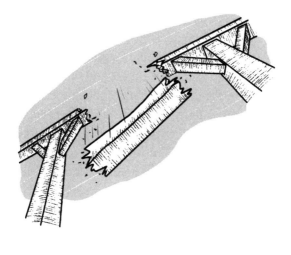

Over the next few weeks, my community rallied around me, bringing me food, helping me heal, and just sitting or walking—very slowly—with me. And unlike the old Tal, I actually *received* their love. I let them help me. I knew I needed it.

"At this point," I told Gia as we walked gingerly along the river bank, "I've fallen off a Rockface while climbing, fallen off a trail while hiking, and fallen while *in* a building. That's got to be some kind of record of clumsiness."

Gia laughed. "I don't think a beam falling on you counts as *you* being clumsy!" She paused and looked carefully at me. "Tal, are you sure you want to go back to work tomorrow? Don't you think your back needs a little more time to heal?"

I knew I was lucky to be walking at all, even though my back ached almost constantly. But I figured getting back into the rhythm of life would help. Even if just to give me some purpose.

"I'll take it slow and ease my way in. I promise."

That's exactly what I tried to do. But no matter how slow I took it, it wasn't slow enough. The pain wouldn't let up. I often found myself distracted, my mind foggy from the pain even as I tried to be present. That terrible voice of shame told me that I should hide how much it hurt, that I should be able to figure it out on my own, and that I shouldn't burden my friends.

But I had followed that voice too many times. I forced myself to instead invite them into my pain, confusion, and frustration. They couldn't fix it, but they could make sure I wasn't alone in it. There were still days I wanted to push them all away and just hide. Kenric was especially good at noticing when I was sliding in that direction.

One day I was staring blankly at some blueprints. I couldn't get my mind to focus. I was exhausted from being in pain all the time, and it seemed like no one could figure out exactly what was wrong—or how to fix it.

I crumpled the paper, my anger and frustration threatening to break out. Why was this happening to me? Why wasn't I getting better? Where was God in this?

I felt a nudge in my spirit. A thought entered my head, but it felt like something . . . *more* than a thought. It was out of nowhere, yet it felt so clear. I was learning to be curious about promptings like that.

I looked toward the mountain range north of town.

I needed to go see Nahal.

A few hours later I found myself on the road. I felt more resigned and desperate than hopeful. Even though the pain in my back was growing sharper by the step, a smile still formed in the corners of my lips when I saw the guest house in the distance. It fit perfectly with the property.

Nahal was in his usual spot, whittling as he looked out over the hills. I forgot how much I enjoyed seeing him.

"It looks like it's *supposed* to be there, doesn't it?" he said, as if he was reading my mind. He rose to greet me as I gingerly walked up his steps. "It's so good to see you, Tal." He then caught a better look at my face and frowned. "What's going on? What's wrong?"

"It's . . . my back," I said, embarrassed at how simple it sounded when it felt anything but.

"Okay," he nodded, clearly concerned. "Well, come on in and tell me the story."

A large cup of coffee later, I finished by saying, "And then for some reason, I felt like the Spirit was telling me to come see you. I know you're not a physical healer, but . . . " I shrugged. "I don't know. I feel like I've tried everything else." It was hard to keep the note of desperation out of my voice.

Nahal leaned back from the time-worn table, looking thoughtful. "Thanks so much for sharing with me, Tal. I do think I can help you. But I don't think it's in the way you're hoping."

"What do you mean?"

"Well, you're right, I'm no healer. But God keeps bringing me people that are in pain in all kinds of ways. At least, I think that's what he's doing. Like I've told you before, this house is a place for people who need some guidance and care in hard seasons. I'm not sure how long he'll keep bringing me people— you never know how long a season is going to be in your story. Could be a month. Could be fifty years. But I'm trying to be faithful in the meantime, and people keep showing up."

Disappointment and fear rose up in my chest. "Got it."

He gave me a knowing nod. "A bit disappointing, I know."

I sighed. "I just . . . I just want to feel better. I hoped you could do that."

"Yep," he nodded. "I get that. I've been there. For me it wasn't physical, it was emotional." He leaned back and paused. "My wife died about ten years ago. And I would have done any-thing, *anything*, to make that pain go away. I kept asking Jesus to help me and it felt like there was just . . . silence."

I hadn't said it out loud. But I wondered where in the world God was in this pain. Was I being punished? Tested?

Forgotten?

"I didn't see what he was doing," Nahal continued, squint-ing over my shoulder like he was watching it play out again. "I didn't realize that that suffering was creating something new in me. Or maybe the better description is *revealing* something new in me. You said you worked for a farmer when you first came here, right?"

I nodded.

"Well, I often think of suffering like how a seed has to be buried in the darkness. But then something strange and in-credible happens in that darkness. The seed cracks open, and something new and wonderful comes out. Suffering seems to be the same. It's painful, and we don't know how long it will last. It can feel like being broken open. But then, sometimes slowly—sometimes with a flash—something beautiful grows."

I considered his words. "So you're saying my suffering might be something good?" I couldn't help the note of bit-terness in my voice.

"I'm saying that 'we know that suffering produces persever-ance; perseverance, character; and character, hope. And hope does not put us to shame.'[3] Yes, you should keep pursuing healing with your pain. But I would also encourage you to start asking the question, 'What might God be up to in the midst of this?' That question never leads to boring answers."

I decided to move into the guest house while I sought treatment with my back. There was something about simply being in Nahal's presence that made me feel safe and calm even while I had to step back from my current roles and trust Gia to lead the Medical Hall project. I often found myself bored, restless, and frustrated. *God, why are you doing this to me?* It felt unfair.

One day, as Nahal was teaching me how to whittle—and I was discovering that I was terrible at it—I asked him a question that had been swirling around in my mind for a while.

"You said when I first told you about my back pain that you didn't know how long this 'season' would last. What do you mean?"

He blew some shavings off his carved bird. "Well, you know we each have a lot of different destinies and a lot of different stories. There's our daily destiny, which is to love well, seek justice, and walk with God.[4] That's an everyday story, but it plays out differently each day. These daily destinies are vital to revealing the Kingdom.

"But then we have *seasons* of destiny, like your season with the farmer, or your season in Ican, or your season helping these new housing developments. These were each different destinies with different stories.

3. *Romans 5:3-5a (NIV)*
4. *Micah 6:8*

"And then over our *lives* we have destinies that build together from all the other ones, all of our smaller stories coming together like tributaries into a large river. I think sometimes we get glimpses of that big river, the big story. Sometimes we have to trust that God can see it even when we can't.[5] But when we worry too much about our lifetime destiny, we usually end up missing out on our daily destinies. We're so worried about what God's doing overall that we miss that moment to love a friend well or stand up to injustice at the market. And that's really where the magic is."

I stared at my shapeless lump of wood that was slowly becoming even more lumpy. "I wish my current season was a little more exciting."

Nahal laughed. "That's the surest way to miss out." He held the bird up to the light and examined his artwork. "Comparison is the great stealer of joy, Tal. The surest way to miss out on enjoying your story is to compare it to other people's. Our seasons of preparation might be at the same time as someone else's season of suffering or fulfillment. You're walking your own path,

5. *Proverbs 3:5-6; Proverbs 20:24*

Tal. Trust that if God wrote this particular story for you, there's a good reason."[6]

∽

Weeks turned into months as I continued to learn ways to strengthen and heal my back. Some days were better than others. I helped Nahal around his property where I could, and I started sitting with him as different travelers came to share their story and seek his help. Every once in a while, he would just sit back and let me take the reins. This always felt nerve-wracking, but exhilarating too.

One night I was adding a log to the fire as Nahal relaxed in an armchair. A new weary traveler had just gone to bed.

"You know, I used to be always on the go," I reflected as I took my own seat. "I think that's one thing I'm learning in this season. I feel like I'm a little less hurried. I'm enjoying the smaller moments more than I used to." It felt strange to hear the Windsong reverberate at such a normal, non-exciting time. I smiled to myself.

Nahal slapped his knees. "I'm glad to hear it because I have something to share. I'm wondering if it's time you took over this house."

The crackling fire was the only sound for a few shocked seconds. "What do you mean?"

"I mean I think my season in this role is wrapping up. I don't know what's next. I'm feeling the itch to write, but I'm not sure. But I'm definitely feeling like this part of my story is slowly coming to a close."

"But . . . I don't know how to do what you do."

6. *I Corinthians 13:12*

"What is it that I do?" he asked.

"I don't know," I said, flustered. I forced myself to think. "You listen to people, and you remind them who they are. Who God is. You tell stories about your own suffering and story. You share wisdom."

"You mean like you shared with that girl last night about how Jesus is helping you to forgive your dad for not being emotionally present, and how you're slowly learning to show him grace?"

"That was different," I replied automatically.

"No it wasn't, and you know it," he said simply. "You have a gift for this stuff, Tal. You're able to be with people in their pain and not try to fix it, and that's more rare than you realize. One of the most exquisite pieces of experiencing our destiny is letting God teach us more about who we uniquely are in his

Kingdom. I know that he has made me to be a Patient Guide. He gave me those words long ago, and they continue to call me forward. I can feel them right here." He tapped his chest. "I think he is teaching you some things about who you uniquely are. Just think about it. See what the Spirit says."[7]

With that he got up and went to bed. I stared at the fire and listened to the Windsong for a long time.

7. *Psalm 119:73*

Guide Notes

What if Jesus designed you as *you* on purpose?

And who knows whether you have not come to the kingdom for such a time as this?

—ESTHER 4:14 (ESV)

As Tal just experienced, there are many different seasons in our journey on the Path. Slowly, they build together with the Master Storyteller weaving our talents, interests, and opportunities together for our unique story.

But, where is Tal's story leading? Where are our stories leading?

Who am I?

We have spent much of our time along the Path returning to this crucial question of, "Because of Jesus, who am I?" We never graduate from this question. As we mature in our walk with Jesus, we begin to see that there are two layers to this question.

Core Identity:

The Crest is your core identity. Your deepest, most foundational, most spectacular identity is as a new, fully-loved, fully-accepted son or daughter of the King of Kings, a precious vessel in whom he lives and through whom he loves. Because of the wondrous work of Jesus, you are now a beloved saint. This core, primary identity can never be lost, altered, or improved upon.

Unique Identity:

Your unique identity combines your particular strengths, weaknesses, passions, interests, and opportunities into a blend that will only ever be worn by you. This is the unique way that *you* are the image of God in this world, the specific and wonderfully personal way he has crafted you to reflect him. You are God's asset in the world, the one he lives in and touches the world through.[8] He fashioned you just as you are for this specific purpose.

8. *Romans 12:4-8*

Throughout your life, the Windsong will sing to you, helping you see the specific ways God has made you *you* and how he intends to use that for deep good. The more you listen to the Windsong, the more you will get to sing *your song*—the melody God specially created for you to sing.

> » **Your unique identity will grow and change over your life**. Unlike our core identity, which never changes, our unique identity will evolve over time, collecting together our experiences, encounters, revelations, and sufferings.
> » **Your unique identity is a gift.** We can be tempted to take ownership of our unique identity, thinking that it depends on us or is a product of our own dedication. But our unique reflection of God is a gift from him just like our core identity. Beware the pride that wants to creep into this area.[9]
> » **Discovering and experiencing your unique identity takes intentionality.** Unearthing the particular ways God has crafted us takes sincere effort. Healthy introspection is not easy, nor is inviting others to speak into our lives, honing our strengths, or owning our weaknesses. The journey of understanding our unique identity is an active, adventurous one!
> » **Shame will try to keep you from experiencing your unique identity.** The enemy hates for us to understand who God has made us. He will try to use our past wounds and deep lies to keep us from stepping into the glorious purposes of God. Bring these wounds and lies to Jesus. Ask him to replace them with his truths.

9. *Ephesians 2:8-9*

God has so much for you, and the enemy will use his favorite weapon of shame to keep you from it.

» **Your unique identity never supersedes your core identity.** It is all too easy for us to begin to disregard or discount the power of our core Crest and begin to place our weight mostly on our unique identity. This is reversing their proper order. Remember: your core identity as a beloved child is always more important and more powerful than any particular strength, talent, or opportunity.

What is my calling?

Just as we have a core identity and a unique identity, we have a core calling and a unique calling.

Core Calling:

God is the Caller.[10] Do you remember Jesus' first call to you, inviting you to trust him and follow him into the unknown? God first and most importantly calls us to follow him, trust him, and be in friendship with him. This is always our core calling in any season and situation. If in doubt, always return to this call to trust.

10. John 6:44; Acts 9:1-9; Romans 8:30

Unique Calling:

Jesus' second call combines your time in history, your circumstances, your relationships, your culture, your financial position, and all the pieces of your life—even your mistakes. God generously sees to the weavings of your unique story. He's been working on a dream for you since before you were born.[11] He knows you could leave the world a better place than when you entered because he designed you for this very purpose.

» **God uses our mistakes**. We *all* carry mess-ups, and these in no way disqualify us from the dreams God has for us. Many times, God uses these mistakes as integral pieces in our calling, redeeming them in ways we never could've imagined.

» **God does not give us clarity in every season.** We will have seasons where we begin to wonder what in the world God is up to, or if there's any purpose in our lives. We may feel left out or forgotten. Relax. Breathe. Sometimes God doesn't give us clarity because his higher priority is that we learn to *trust* him with what is in front of us, so we don't confuse our life purpose as being more important than our friendship with him.

» **God's definition of impact is far greater than ours.** God alone can see and understand all that goes into your unique calling. You may find yourself worrying about whether your call will be impressive enough or impactful enough, or you may judge your calling against what you see in others' lives. Again, relax. Breathe. There are many ripples we will not see this

11. *Jeremiah 1:5*

side of heaven, and many outcomes we may only get faint glimmers of. Trust him. Your destiny is always greater than your potential.[12]

» **God's unique calling on our lives is always for others.** Your unique calling is not primarily for you, but to serve others.[13] Even though we've been given a new selfless Jesus-heart, sometimes we become more concerned about how great or not great we're doing in our lives, forgetting that the call of our lives is to bless others. Jesus calls us to reorient to this truth of serving others just like he did.[14]

» **Calling is not about an assignment, a job, or a vocation.** You may have ten or more "assignments," or jobs, in your lifetime. Try out all of them. Do your best with every assignment, as God will use these to take you more clearly into your calling. Calling is much more all-encompassing than merely an assignment or even a job. Calling is the purpose for which you were made.[15] God will use most or all of your assignments to form your unique calling. There is a through line to God's design for your life, which no formal education or formal assignment can take you into—a storyline that reveals how God designed you to love others, to see them transformed, and to leave this world a better place than when you arrived. God has such a plan for you. Trust him.

12. *Jeremiah 29:11*
13. *1 Peter 4:8-11*
14. *Mark 10:43; John 15:12-13; Acts 20:35*
15. *Isaiah 43:1*

How Do I Discover My Unique Identity and Calling?

You may find yourself asking, "But how do I begin learning more about how God has uniquely crafted and called me?" Here are three practical ways:

1. **Practice some form of listening exercise to hear the Windsong.** Use any practice which fits your temperament. This may be extended time in prayer, seeking solitude, going for a hike, or something else. Intentionally seek out circumstances that help you to listen to the Caller. Ask God how he sees you. Confess to him the lies that hold you back from believing him, and ask him to replace them with truth. Ask him to help you see the unique ways he has created you. Then give yourself time and quiet to listen. He speaks differently to each of us. Be intentional about the spiritual practices which help *you* connect with the Spirit of God. As Jesus said, "He, the Spirit, will lead you into all truth."[16]

2. **Nurture a group of trusted friends who increasingly know you.** True and trusted friends can offer you counsel on how they see you, how they believe the gifts and passions God has put in you were meant to serve his purposes of love, and encourage you along the rocky parts of the Path. Remember,

16. John 16:3

humility is "trusting God and others with me."[17] If you trust such a group of close friends who are for you, who have your back, and who see you for who you are, you will be blessed in ways you cannot imagine. We rarely see ourselves as accurately as a cluster of friends who really know us. They carry serious wisdom for our lives. Ask them what they see in you. Invite them into your journey of discovery.

3. **Reflect on your own story, strengths, and passions.** Introspection and reflection on your own journey can also reveal many clues you may have missed while living your story. There are many helpful ways to engage with this. Talking our stories through with a friend, counselor, or mentor can guide us. So, too, can tools and assessments that provide helpful data points. There are many such tools that help us assess our strengths, passions, giftings, and more. These can be helpful handholds as you reflect on the story God has been weaving for you.

Suffering

We can't leave a discussion about our calling without talking about suffering. Suffering will be a part of all of our journeys just like it was part of Jesus'. It is both a natural consequence of living in a broken world and also an area where God tends to speak most tenderly to us—and we are able to hear him in

17. Lynch, McNicol, and Thrall, *The Cure, Third Edition* (Trueface, 2016) 8, 59, 126, 127, 135

new ways. Suffering, like Nahal shared, allows God to reveal things in us and to us that we cannot access when life feels buttoned-up or straight-forward.[18] As C.S. Lewis said, "God whispers to us in our pleasures, speaks in our conscience, but shouts in our pains: it is His megaphone to rouse a deaf world."[19]

Do not be surprised when suffering comes your way. God wastes nothing. And he often uses our suffering to reveal more of himself and more of us.

When suffering appears on your doorstep, welcome him as best you can. Make him a cup of tea. Ask what he might teach you about your Father or yourself. Many have discovered powerful pieces of their unique calling and identity in seasons of suffering.

Living into Your Story

Frederick Buechner sums up much of what you have been learning all the way along the Path:

> In the entire history of the universe, let alone in your own history, there has never been another day just like today, and there will never be another just like it again. Today is the point to which all your yesterdays have been leading since the hour of your birth. It is the point from which all your tomorrows will proceed until the hour of your death. If you were aware of how precious today is, you could hardly live through it. Unless you are aware of how precious it is, you can hardly be said to be living at all.[20]

18. John 16:33; I Peter 5:10; II Corinthians 4:17
19. C.S. Lewis, The Problem of Pain (HarperCollins, 2001), 91
20. Frederick Buechner, Whistling in the Dark: A Doubter's Dictionary (HarperOne, 1993), 106.

Long before you first met Jesus, before the foundation of the world itself, God was preparing for you. He designed you—yes, *you,* with all your unique quirks and talents and befuddling weaknesses—for such a time as this.

He wrote the music for your story at the start of time and will spend your whole life teaching you to sing it with him.

We do not have to worry that our humanness will overcome his God-ness. Our mistakes and unsure steps are nothing compared to his purposes and plans. In fact, he has taken these very much into account, and will show you how he is turning them into the kind of good you couldn't have dreamed up. No bad day, left turn, or flat-on-our-face failure will change who we are and whose we are.

We are beloved daughters and sons.

We are delighted-in saints.

We are indwelt temples of the holy, living God.

So listen for the song he has been singing to you, and trust the Singer. He knows how to tune your ear. Shake off the shackles of fear and control. They do not belong to you anymore. You are made for the freedom of great love. Jesus does not call us to "Go and work." He does not say, "Go and worry." Nor "Go and fear."

No.

He calls us, throughout the ages . . . "Go and live."

∞

"We're officially open for business," Aran says, his nerves obvious.

I run my hand over the new wooden sign that reads, "Kingdom Builders." I simultaneously think it's cheesy and absolutely wonderful.

I breathe in the morning air. *I can't believe I'm back here.*

The streets of Ican are just waking up, the buzz and bustle of the city stirring like a sleepy hive. I've spent years as the host of Nahal's house—which some called the Room of Grace. But eventually, I began to feel the uncomfortable pull of the Spirit's Windsong. It would have been easier to stay. And I don't believe God would've been mad or disappointed in me if I had. But I also knew he was inviting me into so much more—into the wild adventure of trusting him with my next steps.

Years ago, in front of that fire after Nahal had suggested I take over the house, I had first heard him whisper:

You are my Valiant Builder.

I place my hand over my heart, feeling it beat a little faster at the words. Each day Jesus teaches me more about not only who he is, but who I, uniquely, am. A builder not only of physical structures that help provide safety and stability, but a builder of people, helping them use and refine their unique gifts and talents. What fathomless grace. What astounding love.

It took a while to confide in my friends; half because I wasn't sure what God was really saying, and half because I knew they would encourage me and challenge me with it.

I certainly got that right. I laugh to myself as I watch Gia straightening the drawing tacked up on our wall, Kenric sweeping for the fourth time. Part of me still can't believe they came with me. Part of me suspects that was God's plan all along.

My parents should be here tomorrow for their first visit in years. I've been writing them letters, telling them about the Path. I close my eyes briefly. *Jesus, help their hearts be open. I have so much to share with them.*

"Tal." A voice pulls me out of my reverie. I turn.

"Ricard!" I reach out to shake his hand, genuinely glad to see him. His tone is cool, cautious.

"I heard through the grapevine you were back in town." He looks around our sparsely furnished office. "Glad to see you're still using your talents in some way."

"Yeah," I reply, laughing, "it's been a long road. I'd love to tell you about it sometime."

He nods noncommittally. I don't mind. "So will you be taking students?"

"Eventually." I shrug. "I think we need to get on our feet a little first."

"Well, I have a student—or I *had* a student." He brushes some invisible dust off his coat. "She's incredibly talented, but recently she seems to have lost her way. She's unfocused. Her drawings are suffering. It seems like she can't take the pressure. I thought of you." He glances over, and I'm not sure if he means it as an insult or a compliment. "I've had to cut her from the Guild. But . . . perhaps you could do something with her."

I break into a wide grin. "I'd love that, Ricard. I think I know what she's going through. Please feel free to send her my way."

He nods and turns to walk out. Pausing as he opens the door, he calls over his shoulder, "I'm glad you're back, Tal."

As he walks down the road, I follow to stand in the doorway, watching him disappear into the crowd.

"Adventurously expectant, Jesus!" I exclaim quietly as the Windsong sweeps through the bright streets, bringing the melody of love and grace to Ican.

Selah

Go and live.

Go and live!

You are free, you are new, you are loved!

You are made for glory and good
and deep joy!

You are safe to try and fail and dream and belt
out the song of your life as your
Father surrounds
and sustains
and sings over you.

Go and live!

Name Meanings:

TAL - From "Talitha, cumi" in Mark 5:41, meaning "little lamb" in Aramaic.

RICARD - German name meaning "powerful, strong ruler."

KENRIC - Celtic name meaning "greatest champion."

INGRID - Old Norse name, combining the German god of peace with "beautiful."

GIA - Italian name meaning "God is gracious."

ARAN - Hebrew name meaning "mountain of strength."

NAHAL - Hebrew name meaning "to lead, guide, to give rest to, to refresh."

ROHI - From Jehovah Rohi in Psalm 23:1, meaning "the Lord is my Shepherd."

RAPHA - From Jehovah Rapha in Exodus 15:26, meaning "the Lord is my Healer."

ABBA - Aramaic for Papa or Father.

The
PATH
Experience

Dive deeper into *The Path* with *The Path Experience*, an eight-session small group guide! As you travel alongside Tal's story, you and your group will navigate thought-provoking videos, meaningful discussion questions, practical applications, and reflective exercises. This is more than just a guide—it's an expedition to explore your relationship with God and build authentic connections with others. Whether you're new to faith or seeking to rekindle your passion, *The Path Experience* invites you to chart a course for deeper spiritual discovery and shared growth.

Your next step on the journey starts here—are you ready?

Acknowledgements

We could not be more grateful for the countless voices, perspectives, edits, and passion that have spoken into this project. This entire work is the result of you, our Trueface Tribe, trusting us with your stories, pain, hope, and incredible trust in the God of the Universe. We are humbled.

We want to thank the Trueface writers and thought leaders who have gone before us, especially John Lynch, Bruce McNicol, and Bill Thrall, whose teachings and metaphors in *The Cure* laid the groundwork for the path Tal gets to travel. Thank you for your incredible work.

To our two incisive and precise developmental editors, Katharyn Blair and David Gregory, thank you for making this story actually make sense. Katharyn, you helped add color and heart to this story, bringing Tal to life. David, you added clarity and nuance to the Guide Notes in a way that helps us grasp the depth of the gospel. Thank you both.

Thank you to Pat Malone of Outskirts Studio, who was more than a designer in this project but a vital team member and partner. Pat, your skill helped us see Tal's world for ourselves. Thank you to Abby Wills, who wrangles us into proper grammar and ensures our words get to sing. Thank you to all our beta readers who gave us their time, insights, and perspectives on Tal's story. Thank you to our faithful and committed board members, who let us run hard after dreams and pray for us as we go. Your faithfulness is what has made this project possible.

And last—thank *you*. Wherever you are sitting and reading these words, thank you for traveling with us. Thank you for sticking with Tal, for entering the Cave of trust, for embarking on a journey when you weren't entirely sure where it would lead. We pray that it has led you to the One who is the Author of all great adventures. Grace to you.

Author Bios

ROBBY ANGLE

Robby serves as the President and CEO of Trueface. He and his wife, Emily, are parents to eight children, living in Dawsonville, GA. Previously, they served with Samaritan's Purse in Pakistan and Myanmar, leading international disaster response teams. Robby later directed Adult Ministry Environments and Men's Groups at North Point Community Church in Atlanta for over seven years. He holds a Master's in Community Counseling from Appalachian State, a business degree from the University of Florida, and a Certificate in Biblical Studies from Dallas Theological Seminary.

BRITTANY COULSON

Brittany serves as the Director of Content for Trueface and as a Licensed Associate Counselor for the Mederi Group in Phoenix, Arizona. She specializes in individuals who have undergone trauma, particularly those in their twenties. Previously, Brittany worked internationally as a conservationist and continues to be passionate about the mental health needs of those who care for the earth. She holds a degree in biology from Pepperdine University, a Masters in Conservation Science from Imperial College London, and a Masters in Counseling from Arizona State University.

BENJAMIN CRAWSHAW

Benjamin serves as the Director of Member Engagement for Trueface. Previously, he has headed up the content development for The Rocket Company, a church resourcing organization, as well as leading the student initiative (XP3 Students & High School Camp) at the reThink Group. Prior to this, Benjamin also served as the Creative

Director of High School Ministry at North Point Community Church. He holds a degree in English from Lee University in Cleveland, TN.

BRUCE McNICOL

Dr. Bruce McNicol serves as the founding partner and President Emeritus of Trueface. Leaders in all spheres of influence have found God's lasting resolution for their life issues and key relationships as they have journeyed with Bruce. With degrees in finance law, theology, leadership, and organizational development, Bruce's gifting to write to diverse readers and leaders has proved true in the best-sellers he has co-authored, including *The Cure, The Ascent of a Leader, Bo's Café* and others. Audiences in various countries continue discovering hope and freedom from Bruce's story-driven, biblically-anchored teaching.

About Trueface

Since 1995, Trueface has equipped people to discover the joy and peace of living beyond the mask and building trust in God and others. **It is our prayer to see a world transformed by followers of Jesus experiencing the freedom of living fully alive.**

Today's culture has perfected the art and science of creating masks. Behind these masks, people are dying inside. They're disconnected with God and others. We're here to change that! **Our mission is to equip people to understand who God says they are and experience authentic community.**

We hope to be a bridge for individuals and groups to encounter the peace and freedom of the original good news by trusting God and others with their whole selves. **Our vision is to see tens of thousands of high-trust communities connecting relationally and growing spiritually.**

Join the Trueface Community in the **Trueface Life App** (available in the App Store or Google Play store) to access more free resources, books, studies, and connect with others living the Trueface life. You can also find us on social media:

 Instagram: **@truefacelife**

Facebook: **@truefacecommunity**

Download the Trueface Life App

ᛘTRUEFACE

Books

THE CURE
Unpacking our view of ourselves and our view of God, *The Cure* invites you to remove your mask and experience God's lavish grace. This flagship book explores identity, community, sin, healing, destiny, and more as you discover that maybe God isn't who you think he is...and neither are you.

THE CURE FOR GROUPS
Do you want the kind of small group people will talk about the rest of their lives? A practical guide to starting (or re-igniting) your group, *The Cure for Groups* unpacks five Core Components to build a group that's bursting with life, depth, and the kind of life-changing community Jesus modeled for us.

THE CURE AND PARENTS
Travel with the Clawson family on their summer vacation as they struggle to navigate their family dynamics. Told partly through narrative and partly through teaching, this resource is for anyone wanting to bring grace to their family.

TRUST FOR TODAY

This 365-day devotional invites you to experience grace in your daily life, both in the big moments and the details of life. Use these short readings to incorporate grace into your everyday.

THE ASCENT OF A LEADER

Become the leader people want to follow by opening yourself up to the influences that develop character: enduring relationships with friends, family and God. *The Ascent of a Leader* guides you through cultivating extraordinary character in your home, company, community, and every other arena of life.

BO'S CAFE

When high-powered executive Steven Kerner's bottled pain explodes in his marriage, his carefully curated life crumbles, and he's forced to confront the emptiness beneath his success. *Bo's Café* is a journey of healing, friendship, and the transformative power of grace for anyone longing for a more authentic and fulfilling life.

Small Group Studies

TWO ROADS

Explore the first three chapters of *The Cure* in-depth with this small group study. *Embark* is designed to help your group travel beyond the mask and start experiencing real, authentic relationships through videos, discussion questions, scripture and application.

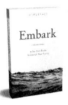

EMBARK

Our resource for starting a transformational small group, *Embark* is the companion group guide to *The Cure for Groups.* Through videos, discussion questions, and practical group applications, it guides you in creating a small group that's bursting with life, depth, and the kind of authentic community Jesus created us for.

CRAZY-MAKING

Have you ever kept doing something you don't want to do? We all have these patterns in our lives that we just can't seem to shake. In this four-week study, you'll explore where these patterns come from, why we keep repeating them, and how to stop the crazy and live in the freedom Jesus made possible. **Based on *The Cure*, Chapter 4.**

HEALING RELATIONSHIPS

We all have experienced the pain of broken relationships, whether we hurt others or they hurt us. While many of us have been told to forgive or repent through gritted teeth and willpower, few of us have been shown how to offer forgiveness or repentance that overflows from our new hearts. Explore the path to freedom and healing Jesus provides in this four-part group study. **Based on *The Cure*, Chapter 5.**

DIVIDED WE STAND

How do you love people when you disagree with them? It can be hard to know how to engage with each other when the gap between us feels like it's widening. Jesus modeled what it looks like to love across political, gender, religious, and cultural lines, and he calls us to do the same. This 4-part group study explores how to follow Jesus in loving people with whom you disagree.

THE HEART OF MAN PARTICIPANT GUIDE

With contributions from Jackie Hill Perry, Dan Allender, WM Paul Young, Jay Stringer and John and Stasi Eldredge, this Trueface resource guides your group through unpacking and processing *The Heart of Man* movie and how to experience the love of the Father in the midst of our darkest struggles.